Grillin' Wild

Max & Maia,
go wild grillin
them critters ~

Rick Browne

Grillin' Wild

with RICK BROWNE

LYONS PRESS
Guilford, Connecticut

An imprint of Globe Pequot Press

Lyons Press is an imprint of Globe Pequot Press.
Interior photos by Rick Browne; photo of author on page vi by Milan Chuckovich
Design: Sheryl P. Kober
Project editor: Julie Marsh
Layout: Nancy Freeborn

Library of Congress Cataloging-in-Publication Data

Browne, Rick, 1946-
  The grillin' wild cookbook : innovative recipes for hunters, fishermen, and outdoor enthusiasts / Rick Browne.
      p. cm.
  Summary: "The companion book to Browne's new show Grillin' Wild on the Sportsmen Channel, about cooking what you catch, shoot, and fish out of waters. It features mouthwatering, gourmet recipes for big game, small game, fowl, and fish, so whether you're looking for the perfect recipe for that giant elk (Chargrilled Elk Tenderloin with Red Miso BBQ Sauce) or a new way to cook that halibut you just caught (Cedar Plank Halibut), The Grillin' Wild Cookbook is chock full of new and tasty ideas"-- Provided by publisher.
  ISBN 978-0-7627-7379-4 (pbk.)
  1. Barbecuing. 2. Cooking (Game) 3. Cooking, American. 4. Cookbooks. I. Title.
  TX840.B3B763 2012
  641.7'6dc23
                                                                              2011037670

Printed in the United States of America

10 9 8 7 6 5 4 3 2 1

Contents

Preface

First, let's get this out of the way right away: I'm not an experienced hunter, fisherman, wing shooter, backwoodsman, or outdoorsman! I am, however, a pretty good chef, a confirmed foodie, and someone who LOVES to cook and eat wild game, waterfowl, upland birds, and fish from both the brine and the brook.

I have spent ten years traveling the United States and through twenty-six countries, authoring ten cookbooks; penning culinary articles for numerous magazines and websites; sampling exotic and nonexotic, wild and domestic culinary fare; and collecting thousands of recipes—all the while talking and sharing kitchen lore and lies with chefs, pitmasters, cooks, and anyone who lives to eat (as opposed to those who merely eat to live).

Up until the age of fifty-four, I had never hunted or fished. It's a shame, too, since my childhood and teen years were spent in Michigan, perhaps the deer-hunting capital of the world and home to great pheasant hunting. I also didn't fish in any of the myriad small lakes or the very big Great Lakes that surround Michigan. So my writing here, and the recipes I've developed or collected herein, aren't from the woodsman perspective, but rather from the view of someone who loves to cook and who, not to blow my own horn, has been told on several occasions that I can "cook up a storm."

Although not born with a rifle, shotgun, or fishing pole in my hand, I have taken gun safety courses and trap/skeet-shooting lessons; have a bunch of fly-fishing lessons under my belt; have heeded the advice of professional guides, experienced hunters, and fishermen; always do my homework before hunting trips; and practice that aspect of being in the wild that is perhaps most important: using common sense. If I don't know something about hunting or fishing, I ask; if I haven't done something, I ask someone to show me how; and if in doubt, I let the pros take over.

Whether it's cooking a moose brisket for thirty-six hours, braising a whole pheasant with honey-garlic sauce, or cedar-planking a whole salmon, folks say I know my way around the kitchen or barbecue. Thanks. I work very hard at it.

My hunting and fishing experiences began with my hosting *Ready, Aim . . . Grill* on the Outdoor Channel, where, as they say, I experienced an epiphany of sorts. I found that I loved heading into the forest with a rifle to look for white-tailed deer, thrilled at tracking wild boar in the foothills of Texas, delighted in grabbing a shotgun and sitting for hours in a blind in the rain waiting for pintails or mallards, and relished every second of my fishing expeditions in the Pacific off Mexico and British Columbia as much as learning how to fly fish for sturgeon and salmon on the Kennebec River in Maine.

So I decided to bring my chef skills to hunting and fishing, rather than the other way around. I have a dozen years of experience in the kitchen, and only a few in the field and stream. But who would you rather cook a buffalo prime rib for you? Someone who knows the muzzle velocity of a .270 Winchester and the mating habits of moose, or someone who can turn a tough, old, wild tom turkey into the most tender roast bird you've ever laid your gums on?

I'm a chef who hunts and fishes. Welcome to my table.

Rick Browne

Introduction

What we cook and the way we cook has seen many changes over the last 30,000 years. We've exchanged a T. rex bone for a T-bone—and that may not be the best choice man has made.

What began as a caveman tearing off a raw piece of mammoth later became throwing a hunk of musk ox or saber-toothed tiger directly onto fiery coals to char it for dinner. Today those cavefolks' distant relatives can place a steak in a microwave or convection oven and cook it perfectly within minutes. No charcoal or cinders to wipe off their rib eyes.

As with any method or style of cooking worth its salt (or today a salt substitute), changes are inevitable, as new tools, techniques, meats, vegetables, fruits, and even spices and herbs are discovered, formulated, and enter today's kitchens.

I've noticed that health concerns, most prompted by the zillions of articles published about the detriments of fast food, and the plethora of processed and packaged "convenience foods" are causing people to change what they cook (for example, away from burgers, hot dogs, and ribs) and, in more than a few cases, are going back in time with their diets.

Don't worry, velociraptor cutlets or mammoth burgers won't appear on your local restaurant menu any time soon, but folks are looking more to the wild for sources of protein. They're eagerly cooking up bison, venison, elk, rabbits, rattlesnakes, wild boar, antelope, and other meats that our foreforeforeforefathers consumed—hopefully, with a few better cooking techniques and recipes.

It seems like a lot of us have gone back to the woods, retracing the culinary steps our ancient ancestors trod around the campfire, as we look toward wild meat and fowl to grill up in our backyards. Between fourteen million and eighteen million US residents participate in hunting in any given year. This represents approximately 5 percent of the US population, who end up spending at least $22.7 billion on hunting each year. That's a lot of folks bringing home the wild boar bacon.

But wait! The renewed interest in and consumption of wild game, game birds, and fish isn't just for the folks who head to the backwoods, prairies, and streams. People who wouldn't know a .20 gauge from a Bowie knife are getting a taste for venison, wild boar, and grouse, and while they don't head to the forests, they either have friends who hunt and generously share their elk or venison or wild goose, or they mosey over to their computers and order rack of elk or antelope medallions or saddle of rabbit online.

And, by the way, the purchase of wild game online has exploded, as annual sales of game bought from various Internet purveyors has skyrocketed from $110 million to $340 million in just a few short years.

"Our growth has doubled in the last five years, averaging almost 20 percent a year," says the owner of an online wild game company in Seattle. "Especially with bison, which seems to be most popular in the western states, but also with rattlesnake, kangaroo, and elk."

Nicky USA, in Portland, Oregon, which has by far the largest selection of game available online, has also seen their sales rocket in the past five years. "As chefs, and home cooks, learn more about how to cook game and the health benefits of foods like bison and ostrich, we've seen a substantial increase in the interest in cooking these at home, and in upscale restaurants," says owner Geoff Latham.

The Nicky USA catalog (ten single-spaced pages long) that you can download contains an incredible list of game. The bison (buffalo) section alone has fifty-four cuts of meat listed, everything from bone-in rib eyes and short ribs to buffalo bull fries. Started as a small company selling rabbits to local restaurants, Nicky's list of wild game and fowl now numbers over one hundred items and is constantly growing.

If you love sausage, you never "sausage" a list of edibles. Nicky has thirty-two varieties, including some intriguing mixtures like smoked duck with apple brandy, buffalo bratwurst with burgundy wine, and pheasant with cognac and hazelnuts.

And if you're a burger aficionado, these wild game sites offer burgers made from eleven different species for your tasting pleasure, including alligator, yak, goat, and kangaroo.

Ordering game online does come with one disadvantage—cost. Since all game meats are perishable, and regulations require a maximum of two-day shipping, costs for those antelope steaks and buffalo burgers can be very high. But since you're probably not going to be ordering exotic meat every week, or even every month, the higher costs can be tolerated. Also, several of the online companies are working on getting two-day UPS service at a reduced rate for food items. Your best bet is to check with the company you're buying from before you click that final "Purchase Products" button on the screen.

Although the cost of game ordered online may be higher than regular beef or pork or chicken, people are finding not only a significant taste difference, but also tremendous health benefits, particularly in the case of bison.

"Bison fat contains four times the folic acid of any other animal," shares Skip Sayers, who owns American Gourmet (http://americangour

met.net), yet another website dedicated to wild game meats. One medical study found that eating three four-ounce portions of bison a week for twenty-four weeks resulted in participants' LDL [bad cholesterol] level dropping by 45 percent.

Sayers adds, "Scientists also did a study of Native American Plains Indians and found that while some died of tuberculosis and other infectious diseases, they never found any evidence of cancer or heart or stroke problems. And their diet consisted mainly of bison."

While restaurants are restricted by law from selling "wild game," they are selling farm-raised game in steadily increasing numbers. Elk, buffalo, venison, rabbits, wild boar, water buffalo, quail, pheasant, and grouse are some of the game available.

Heck, even my local grocery store has buffalo for sale several times a year, and rabbit is usually available. I'm hoping it won't be long until they add venison, wild boar, and elk to their meat shelves. Nearby, several upscale restaurants are putting farm-raised venison, wild boar, pheasant, quail, and even elk on the menu. It's only going to get better as more and more folks seek out low-fat and preservative- and chemical-free game to replace fattier, chemically enhanced beef and pork.

Then there are the cookbooks. Gradually chefs, cooks, and cookbook authors are getting it—wild game-wise, that is. The number of wild game cookbooks has steadily increased over the last five to ten years, and great ones (like this humble tome) are encouraging people to cook up what neighbor Jim brought back from his moose hunt, or to go online and order buffalo prime rib for their next dinner party.

But cooking Mr. Caribou or Sir Partridge isn't quite the same as roasting a beef rib eye or sautéing a sirloin. As most game meats are low in fat and cholesterol, cooking, especially grilling, can be tricky if not done right. The lack of fat on one hand is good, but fat is what helps add moisture, flavor, and tenderness to meat when it's cooking. Take away the fat, and you must cook smarter; otherwise, your steaks, ribs, and chops will look and taste like old shoe leather.

I highly recommend that you do not cook buffalo, elk, venison, moose, caribou, reindeer, musk ox, antelope, or yak past medium-rare. If you do, you will not like the dry, tasteless results. Cook the meat for a short time over high heat to sear in the juices, then move it to an indirect (unheated) side of the grill, often over a water pan to prevent dripping fat from igniting and to add moisture to what you are cooking, and finish cooking until you reach medium-rare.

Canada goose looks and tastes remarkably like a beef tenderloin; buffalo prime rib is far more flavorful and healthy than its beef counterpart, and knocks beef prime rib off the pedestal; and a sandwich made of pulled pork from a wild boar (properly flavored and cooked) is an identical twin to a sandwich made from domestic pork,

despite the fact that one pig lived a pampered life on a ranch, while the other literally had to fight and scrape for every morsel of food.

You can, of course, stew meats, or brine or marinate them to add moisture, or wrap them in bacon to add fat and moisture. But those techniques, especially the bacon trick, adds fat loaded with cholesterol. A simpler answer is to just cook it right.

One thing to remember, whether you bring game home yourself from a hunting trip, are given it by a friend or neighbor who hunts, or have your rack of wild boar delivered by UPS, wild game is absolutely organic. No tenderizers, antibiotics, vitamins, steroids, or flavor enhancers are in your moose burger or venison roast.

Try saying that about the prepackaged, colored, water-infused, chemical-saturated meats you buy in your local supermarket.

That, my friends, is meat we should be terrified of.

Big Game

Fire-Grilled Antelope Steak

Rinse antelope steaks in cold water to help reduce what can be a slightly bitter taste from the grains and wild grasses they eat. Antelope is milder in flavor than elk or some venison cuts and very tender and flavorful. If someone doesn't like the "gameyness" of other large game, encourage them to try antelope steaks or chops.

Serves 6–8

¾ cup fresh lemon juice
¼ cup chopped yellow onion
1 teaspoon chopped fresh garlic
¼ cup olive oil
¼ teaspoon kosher salt
¼ teaspoon celery seeds
½ teaspoon onion powder
½ teaspoon chopped fresh basil
¼ teaspoon dried savory
1 teaspoon dried rosemary
1 tablespoon minced fresh garlic
Pinch of red pepper flakes

3-pound antelope roast, cut into
    1-inch-thick steaks

Baste
¼ cup olive oil
2 tablespoons balsamic vinegar
2 cloves garlic, finely diced

Pat of butter for each steak

1. In a resealable plastic bag or large shallow bowl, combine all ingredients except meat. Add the meat and shake or stir to coat all pieces, close bag or cover bowl, and refrigerate 5–6 hours (or overnight).

2. Prepare the grill for medium-hot cooking (450°F). Combine olive oil, vinegar, and garlic for the baste; set aside.

3. Place steaks on a well-oiled rack 6 inches above hot coals or gas flames and grill 20–24 minutes, turning once and basting occasionally with the flavored olive oil.

4. When the meat reaches 155°F, remove the steaks from the grill, place a pat of butter on each steak, cover, and let sit 5–10 minutes to recirculate juices in the meat.

5. Serve with red wine, baked potatoes, and grilled vegetables.

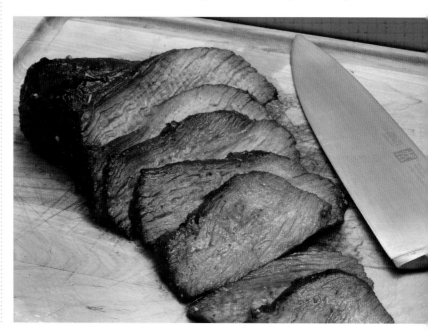

Wyoming Wild Salisbury Steaks

You can also use suet or fatback salt pork in this recipe in place of the ground pork to add a bit of fat and flavor, but if using the salt pork, be sure to rinse it well first. One of the most beautiful and graceful animals on the American Plains, antelope is delicious and, like most game, extremely low in calories.

Serves 4

1. In a medium bowl, mix half of the soup mix into the ground antelope and pork; set aside.

2. In a small bowl, combine bread crumbs, garlic, oregano, pepper flakes, milk, and egg, then add to the meat mixture, stirring well.

3. Form 4 patties and brown them in the oil in a skillet, about 3 minutes per side. Remove patties to a plate.

4. Add flour and remaining soup mix to skillet. Brown and add onions and water; simmer 20 minutes. Return the patties to the skillet and simmer 15 minutes.

5. Serve on plates or on focaccia bread or onion rolls.

1 (2-ounce) package onion soup mix, divided
1 pound ground antelope
¼ pound ground pork
¼ cup seasoned dry bread crumbs
1 teaspoon granulated garlic
1 teaspoon dried oregano
½ teaspoon sweet red pepper flakes
¼ cup whole milk
1 egg, lightly beaten
2 tablespoons olive or corn oil
2 tablespoons flour
1 large onion, sliced into ⅛-inch rings
1½ cups water

Marinated Antelope Leg

As with all game and domestic meat, I prefer to cook the leg "bone-in," as I think it gives the meat more flavor, but you may wish to remove the bone and tie the roast before cooking. Again, I prefer to cook any meat with the bone as most chefs agree the bone in a steak or roast adds flavor. It also transmits heat to the inside of the steak or roast making it easier to cook evenly.

Serves 6–8

Marinade

½ cup olive oil

2 cups Riesling wine

¼ cup fresh lemon juice

2 tablespoons Worcestershire sauce

1 teaspoon garlic salt

1 teaspoon seasoned salt

1 teaspoon freshly ground black pepper

1 teaspoon oregano

1 teaspoon sage

2 tablespoons minced garlic

4-pound antelope leg roast

4 large cloves garlic, sliced

1. In a large resealable plastic bag, mix all the marinade ingredients, then add the leg and seal the bag. Refrigerate at least overnight or up to 36 hours, turning it occasionally to distribute the marinade.

2. Remove the meat from the marinade and drain well, reserving the marinade, and let the meat come to room temperature. Preheat the barbecue or oven to medium-low (250–300°F) for indirect heating, putting a water pan under the roast on the grill rack.

3. In a small saucepan, boil the marinade for 10 minutes. You can then use it to baste the meat.

4. With a small knife, cut slits in the meat and fill each slit with a slice of garlic.

5. Roast the leg for 8 hours, basting occasionally and turning the meat several times. Slice and serve at the table, or chill the roast and serve cold slices for sandwiches or mixed into a green salad.

Antelope Loin with Onion Sauce

You can also use a sweeter onion (Walla Walla, Vidalia, or Maui) in this recipe, but I like the bit of bite that the yellow or white onions bring to the dish.

Serves 4–6

1. Preheat the oven or barbecue grill to medium-high (350–400°F).

2. In a large dutch oven or casserole, heat olive oil over medium-high heat until it begins to smoke. Generously salt and pepper the roast, then place in the pan and brown on all sides.

3. Remove the roast from the pan and set aside. Add onions, carrots, celery, parsley, and green onions to the pan and cook 2–3 minutes while stirring, then add the garlic when the vegetables are wilted and beginning to lightly brown.

4. Return the browned roast to the pan, placing it on top of the cooked vegetables, and place the pan in the preheated oven or barbecue and roast the loin to medium-rare, 15–18 minutes.

5. Remove the roast from the pan and cover with foil.

6. Place the pan over high heat on the stove or barbecue side burner and add the wine; stir to deglaze the pan. Reduce to a sauce-like thickness, then add the orange juice and stock and cook until the liquid is reduced by half.

7. Remove the vegetables with a slotted spoon or by pouring mixture through a strainer into a saucepan. Heat the sauce until it just begins to boil, whisk in butter, and stir to incorporate.

8. Slice the meat into 1/4-inch-thick slices and arrange on a platter. Drizzle with some of the sauce, reserving the rest to serve at the table.

2 tablespoons extra-virgin olive oil
3–4 pound boneless antelope loin
1 tablespoon kosher salt
1 teaspoon freshly ground black pepper
2 large yellow onions, diced
¾ cup diced carrots
¾ cup diced celery
½ cup minced fresh parsley
¼ cup chopped green onions, green and white parts
6 cloves garlic, minced
1 cup hearty red wine (pinot noir or cabernet)
½ cup orange juice
3 cups beef or vegetable stock
3 tablespoons butter

Bear Roast in Whiskey-Raisin Sauce

Many hunters say spring bear meat is best, because the bear has lived on its fat all winter, making the meat far less fatty than that of fall bears, who are building up fat for the winter ahead. In either case, heed the warning about removing ALL fat! The photo below shows the pound of fat that was removed from a 2-pound roast.

Serves 6–8

1. Preheat the oven or barbecue to medium-high (350–400°F).

2. Cut all fat off the bear roast (this is very important, as bear fat can turn bitter and rancid when cooked) and place the trimmed roast in a dutch oven or roasting pan. Pour in water and add onions and carrots. Cover and roast 2½ hours.

3. Mix flour, dry mustard, salt, and pepper in a saucepan. Slowly add lemon juice and whiskey. Add raisins and cook over medium heat, stirring constantly, until mixture has a syrupy consistency.

4. Pour the mixture over the bear roast, then continue to roast 30–40 minutes until the meat is fork tender, basting 3 or 4 times while the roast is cooking.

5. Serve with steamed potatoes with butter and parsley, and grilled acorn squash.

4-pound boneless bear roast
2 cups water
2 large onions, diced
2 carrots, diced
1 tablespoon flour
2 tablespoons dry mustard
½ teaspoon seasoned salt
1 teaspoon freshly ground black pepper
2½ tablespoons fresh lemon juice
1½ cups whiskey
1 cup seedless raisins

Browne's Brown Bear Stew

This recipe comes from my older brother Grant, who lives in British Columbia and is an avid sportsman. While he used to hunt regularly, now he just enjoys hiking and camping in the wondrous environs of Canada's Rocky Mountains. He is always willing to share his recipes.

Serves 4–6

¼ cup olive oil

1 pound bear meat, roast (boneless) or steaks, cut into 1-inch pieces

1½ cups beef broth

1 cup red wine (optional)

1 large leek, white part only, thinly sliced

3 large carrots, sliced

1 large onion, sliced

2 cloves garlic, minced

3 stalks celery, chopped

3 medium Yukon Gold potatoes, cubed

½ pound mushrooms, chopped

½ cup dried cranberries (Craisins)

1 (14.5-ounce) can chopped tomatoes

½ teaspoon kosher salt

½ teaspoon freshly ground black pepper

2 teaspoons dried savory

1 teaspoon dried oregano

1. Put oil in a dutch oven and, over high heat, add the bear meat, stirring it well to brown evenly on all sides. Do this in two or three batches so the pan won't be overcrowded, which can result in uneven browning.

2. Add broth and red wine (if using), then add vegetables, potatoes, mushrooms, cranberries, and canned tomatoes. Stir to incorporate, then add salt, pepper, savory, and oregano.

3. Turn down the heat and simmer 1½–2 hours, stirring often and adding more liquid if necessary to keep the vegetables and meat covered.

4. When the meat is fork tender, remove the pot from the burner and bring to the table to ladle into wide soup bowls. Serve with grilled garlic bread and a glass of burgundy, merlot, or cabernet.

Curried Bear Meatballs

This recipe is for meatballs, but you can use the exact same recipe to make bear sausages, mixing the ingredients and then stuffing them inside sausage casings. Make sure to cook the sausages or meatballs thoroughly—you do not want to see any pink in any cooked bear meats.

Serves 8–10

4 pounds ground bear meat
2 pounds ground pork butt
8 slices bacon, finely chopped
2 teaspoons red pepper flakes
2 tablespoons freshly minced garlic
2 tablespoons kosher salt
1 tablespoon freshly ground black pepper
2 tablespoons curry powder
2 large eggs, lightly beaten
2 tablespoons whiskey
2 cups dry bread crumbs

1. In a large bowl, mix the bear, pork butt, and bacon thoroughly with your hands, making sure that everything is well combined.

2. In a separate bowl, combine the red pepper flakes, garlic, salt, black pepper, curry powder, eggs, whiskey, and bread crumbs, again mixing thoroughly.

3. Add the bread crumb mixture to the meat and, again using your hands, mix together. Form golf ball–size meatballs from the mixture.

4. Either fry the meatballs in olive oil or bake in a wide, flat casserole or dutch oven. Fry for 10–12 minutes, turning often, or bake for 30 minutes at 350°F, in either case using a meat thermometer to make sure internal temperature is 160°F.

5. Serve the meatballs with your favorite barbecue sauce, or put them in a saucepan of spaghetti sauce and warm up to serve as pasta and bear meatballs.

Bruin Meat Loaf

Most bears have parasites in their muscles, so it's important to thoroughly cook any bear meat. While trichinosis has been largely eliminated in pork, wild game—especially bear—can contain the roundworms that carry the disease, which can be extremely hazardous to your health.

Serves 4–6

½ cup minced red bell pepper
1 cup chopped yellow onion
½ cup minced carrots
1 teaspoon marjoram
1 teaspoon curry powder
½ teaspoon chili powder
1 egg, beaten
1 cup ketchup
¼ cup chopped raw bacon
1½ pounds ground bear meat
¼ pound ground pork
1 teaspoon kosher salt
½ teaspoon freshly ground black pepper
¼ teaspoon red pepper flakes
1 (10¾-ounce) can condensed tomato soup

1. Preheat the barbecue or oven to medium-high (350–400°F).

2. In a large bowl, combine all the ingredients except the tomato soup and mix very well with your hands.

3. Form the meat mixture into a cast-iron skillet or meat loaf pan and bake about 1 hour or until meat is firm and reaches an internal temperature of 160°F.

4. After 45 minutes, pour the tomato soup over the top of the meat loaf, spread with a spatula, and continue to cook for about 15 minutes. The soup should be thick and bubbling.

5. Remove the meat loaf from the barbecue or oven, cover, and let rest 10 minutes.

6. Slice meat loaf and serve with garlic mashed potatoes and sautéed green beans.

CB's Bear Chops

I like to serve these chops with steamed new potatoes and a grilled or sautéed vegetable like asparagus or bell peppers. "CB" is our son Chris, who has become, in his adult years, a real foodie.

Serves 4

4 boneless bear chops
¼ cup flour
1 tablespoon onion powder
3 tablespoons bacon fat or olive oil
1 cup Guinness beer
1 (2-ounce) package onion soup mix
1 cup sliced button or crimini mushrooms
1 (10.5-ounce) can golden mushroom cream soup
½ teaspoon garlic salt
1 teaspoon oregano
½ teaspoon freshly ground black pepper

1. Preheat the oven to 350°F.

2. Trim all fat from the chops, then dredge each chop in the flour seasoned with onion powder.

3. In a cast-iron skillet, brown chops on both sides in hot bacon fat or olive oil over medium-high heat (350–400°F).

4. In a small bowl, combine beer, soup mix, mushrooms, mushroom soup, salt, oregano, and pepper and stir to incorporate. Pour over the bear chops.

5. Place chops in the oven and cook 1½ hours, basting occasionally with the liquid in the skillet.

6. Remove from the oven, cover the meat, and let it rest 5 minutes. Serve smothered in the rich mushroom and beer gravy.

Teriyaki Buffalo Burgers

Since most buffalo meat is farm-raised nowadays, you can safely eat steaks, roasts, and burgers that are done to medium-rare. In fact, cooking them much beyond this stage lessens the flavor and moisture of the meat.

Serves 6–8

1. In a small saucepan, combine the marinade ingredients and heat to boiling, then turn off the heat and stir until well mixed. Set aside.

2. Brush pineapple slices with olive oil or spray them with cooking spray, and place them over a medium-hot grill. When they are grill-marked on both sides (about 2 minutes per side), remove them and set aside for garnish.

3. Pour half of the marinade into a 12 x 9 x 3-inch Pyrex dish, reserving the other half for basting.

4. In a large bowl, thoroughly mix the buffalo meat and beaten egg with your hands. Form 6–8 patties and place them in the marinade. Turn them over after 8 minutes and let them soak for another 8 minutes, then remove the patties and discard the marinade.

5. Cook the burgers on the barbecue grill or in a stove-top skillet until cooked through, about 4 minutes per side. Baste occasionally with the remaining marinade, including right before serving.

6. Place the burgers on toasted hamburger buns, add a full slice of grilled pineapple to each burger, and serve.

Marinade
2 tablespoons minced Vidalia (or other sweet variety) onion
1 teaspoon ground ginger
2 tablespoons brown sugar
¼ cup pineapple juice
¼ cup soy sauce
1 teaspoon freshly minced garlic
6–8 thin slices of fresh pineapple
Olive oil

Burgers
2 pounds ground buffalo meat
1 egg, beaten
6–8 hamburger buns or rolls

Grilled Buffalo Rib Eye Steaks with Roquefort Butter

I think that there is no finer steak anywhere than a bone-in buffalo rib eye. Although not as marbled as a beef rib eye, it's loaded with flavor, perfectly moist and juicy (please don't cook beyond medium-rare), and as tender as any steak you'll ever cook. I'm salivating as I write this.

Serves 4–6

1 tablespoon extra-virgin olive oil
4–6 buffalo rib eye steaks,
    1–1¼ inches thick
    (8–10 ounces each)
½ teaspoon kosher salt
Freshly ground black pepper

Roquefort Butter
½ cup unsalted butter, room
    temperature
4–6 tablespoons crumbled
    Roquefort cheese
½ teaspoon finely minced shallots
2 teaspoons brandy
Pinch of kosher salt
Freshly ground black pepper

1. Heat grill to medium (300–350°F or to the point where you can hold your hand 5 inches over the flame for 3–4 seconds) for indirect heating, putting a water pan under the unheated side of the grill.

2. Rub olive oil onto both sides of each steak, and sprinkle each side with salt and pepper.

3. Place steaks on the grill and cook until well browned on one side, 2½–3 minutes per side. Turn steaks and place on the cooler side of the grill 5–6 minutes for rare (120°F on instant-read thermometer), 7–8 minutes for medium-rare (130°F), or 8–9 minutes for medium (135–140°F).

4. While steaks are cooking, mash together the room-temperature butter, crumbled Roquefort cheese, shallots, and brandy. Lightly season with salt and pepper to taste.

5. Remove the steaks from the grill and place them on a heated platter. Top each steak with a generous portion of the Roquefort butter, cover the steaks with foil, and let the meat rest 5 minutes. Serve immediately.

Braised Buffalo ~~Tales~~ Tails

In this recipe I cook and serve the buffalo the same day—after more than six hours of cooking time, that is—but you can also stop the process after you've strained the vegetables from the gravy (step 5), and at that point refrigerate the meat and sauce overnight, resuming the last two hours of cooking the next day. Some say it tastes better this way, but I'm unconvinced.

Serves 4–6

3 tablespoons olive oil
3-pound buffalo tail, cut into
    3-inch pieces
4 cups beef stock
1 (6-ounce) can tomato paste
½ cup merlot
1 large onion, chopped
3 large carrots, chopped
2 stalks celery, chopped
5 sprigs fresh thyme
2 tablespoons freshly
    chopped basil
1 teaspoon freshly minced garlic
⅛ teaspoon ground cloves
¼ teaspoon cinnamon
1–2 tablespoons flour

1. Preheat the oven or barbecue to medium-low (250–300°F) for indirect heating, putting a water pan under the unheated side of the grill. If using an oven, place a water pan on the bottom rack with the meat on the rack above.

2. Pour the olive oil in a large dutch oven and brown the tail sections over medium-high heat (350–400°F) until browned on all sides.

3. In a large bowl, combine the beef stock, tomato paste, merlot, onion, carrots, celery, thyme, basil, garlic, cloves, and cinnamon, and stir well. Pour into the dutch oven over the browned tail sections and bring to a boil over medium-high heat.

4. Cover the dutch oven and cook in the oven or barbecue for 4 hours, stirring occasionally.

5. Remove the pot from the oven or barbecue. Using a slotted spoon, remove the vegetables from the sauce and discard the vegetables, pouring the remaining thin sauce back over the meat. Cook another 2 hours or until the meat easily separates from the bones.

6. Remove the tail sections from the sauce and place them on a heated platter. Add flour, a tablespoon at a time, to thicken the gravy to your taste.

7. Combine the gravy with the tail sections and serve with sautéed turnips and steamed or braised cabbage.

Buffalo Nickel Potpie

To garnish these pies, I use a buffalo-shaped cookie cutter that I ordered from Amazon.com and which I understand is also available at Sears. It costs just over a dollar and creates a wonderful presentation for this dinner. I cut a buffalo shape from a scrap of the pastry, brush it with browning sauce, and put it on top of the crust before placing the dish into the oven.

Serves 4–6

2–3 tablespoons olive oil
1½ pounds bison stew meat,
    cut into ¾-inch cubes
4 teaspoons minced shallots
1 large clove garlic, minced
1½ tablespoons butter
¼ cup flour
½ cup port wine
2 cups beef stock
1 tablespoon tomato paste
½ teaspoon seasoned salt
½ teaspoon freshly ground
    black pepper
1 teaspoon oregano
½ teaspoon marjoram
1 teaspoon savory
½ cup diced carrots
½ cup fresh or frozen corn kernels
½ cup pearl onions
1 sheet frozen puff pastry dough,
    thawed
1 egg
2 tablespoons milk

1. Preheat the barbecue or oven to 300–350°F.

2. Heat olive oil over medium-high heat in a dutch oven or large cast-iron skillet on the stove until it just begins to smoke. Add bison cubes and brown on all sides, then remove the cubes with a slotted spoon and set aside.

3. Add more oil to the dutch oven if necessary and add shallots and garlic. Cook 2–3 minutes until shallots begin to soften, but do not let the garlic burn or turn brown. Return the meat to the dutch oven.

4. In a clean skillet, cook butter and flour over medium heat, stirring constantly, until you have a dark golden brown roux. Add port and stock, then add tomato paste, salt, pepper, oregano, marjoram, and savory, and stir while bringing to a boil.

5. Pour the contents of the skillet over the buffalo meat and put the dutch oven in the barbecue or oven. Cook 2 hours, stirring several times.

6. Remove the dutch oven and add carrots, corn, and pearl onions. Return it to the heat, covered, and cook another 30 minutes.

7. Remove the dutch oven from the heat and divide the stew mixture into two ovenproof dishes—large ceramic ramekins are perfect.

8. Roll out the puff pastry on a floured surface and cut it in half, with each piece large enough to cover a dish. Stretch the pastry over the lip of each dish so that there is an overhang of at least an inch.

9. Beat egg and milk together. Brush the pastry with the egg mixture, and cut vents into the pastry with a sharp knife.

10. Bake in a 375°F oven or barbecue for 30 minutes. Remove pies, cover, and let rest for 10 minutes before serving at the table.

Bison Wellington

If you want to be really elegant, put a thin slice of foie gras on top of each fillet before you fold it in the pastry. The goose liver pâté will partially melt and provides a heavenly flavor to this dish. Or, if you haven't won the lottery, use the chicken liver pâté.

Serves 4

10 tablespoons olive oil, divided
½ onion, chopped
1 teaspoon paprika
¾ cup port wine
½ cup beef stock
2 tablespoons Kitchen Bouquet (or other browning sauce)
2 cloves garlic, minced
1 teaspoon chopped fresh rosemary
½ teaspoon savory
Kosher salt and freshly ground black pepper, divided
¼ cup heavy cream
10 small crimini or button mushrooms, caps only, minced
4 medium shallots, minced
Kosher salt and freshly ground black pepper
½ cup tawny port wine
1 teaspoon Worcestershire sauce
4 (6-ounce) buffalo fillets, trimmed, with trimmings reserved
2 sheets frozen puff pastry dough, thawed
4 (1-ounce) slices chicken liver pâté or fois gras
1 egg yolk
1 tablespoon milk
1 ounce sherry
1 tablespoon butter

1. Heat 3 tablespoons olive oil in a sauté pan over medium heat. Add onion, paprika, port, beef stock, Kitchen Bouquet, garlic, rosemary, savory, and pinches of salt and pepper, and stir while cooking 12–15 minutes. Add heavy cream and cook until the sauce is thick enough to coat the back of a spoon. Remove from heat; cover and keep warm.

2. In a large cast-iron skillet over medium-high heat, sauté mushrooms in 3 tablespoons olive oil for 4–5 minutes. Add shallots, a light sprinkle of salt and pepper, port, and Worcestershire sauce, and cook for another minute or two. Remove the mushrooms and shallots with a slotted spoon to a small bowl; cover and set aside. Reserve the drippings in the pan.

3. Return the pan to the burner and add 2 tablespoons olive oil; heat until oil just begins to smoke, about 3 minutes. Season the fillets with salt and pepper, then place them in the hot skillet and brown on top and bottom.

4. Preheat the oven or barbecue to 425°F.

5. Open 1 sheet of puff pastry dough and cut in half, then stretch the dough slightly and place on a floured cutting board. Place 1 fillet in the center of the dough, top each piece of meat with a slice of pâté and 2 tablespoons of the sautéed mushrooms and shallots, and wrap tightly. Repeat with the other fillets. Beat egg yolk and milk together, and brush each fillet with the egg wash.

6. Put 2 tablespoons olive oil in a cast-iron skillet, add the dough-wrapped fillets (seam side down), and cook in the barbecue or oven for about 25 minutes. Pastry crust should be nicely browned.

7. Remove the Wellingtons, cover with aluminum foil, and let rest 3–5 minutes. The shorter time will result in a rare fillet; the longer time will produce meat that is closer to medium.

8. Warm the sauce in a saucepan and whisk in the sherry and butter. Serve each Wellington on a pool of sauce on a heated plate, with the remaining sauce served on the side.

Rack of Elk

In some recipes you may see elk referred to as "venison"—that's not a mistake. Originally venison was used to describe game animals killed by hunters, including deer, hare, wild pigs, goats, ibex, moose, reindeer, antelope, and elk, but today the word is usually associated with various species of deer. Actually, deer and elk meat can pretty much be substituted for each other in most recipes.

Serves 4

3 tablespoons olive or
   vegetable oil
1 rib rack elk (about 8 bones/chops)
Freshly ground black pepper
1 teaspoon garlic powder
2 tablespoons butter
4 tart apples (Granny Smith or
   Pippin), cored and sliced
½ cup brown sugar
¼ cup balsamic vinegar
½ cup hearty red wine
2 tablespoons crushed Szechuan
   peppercorns
½ cup beef stock

1. Heat oil in a dutch oven or roasting pan over medium heat until hot. Season elk with pepper and garlic powder and sear the rack 2–3 minutes on all sides. Lift out the rack, put it on a platter, and cover with foil. Discard all but 1 tablespoon of the oil.

2. Preheat the barbecue or oven to medium-high (350–400°F).

3. Pour the tablespoon of oil and 2 tablespoons butter into a deep saucepan over medium-high heat. When the butter stops foaming, add the apples, sautéing until they begin to caramelize and turn brown, about 3–4 minutes. Add sugar and vinegar and cook another 1–2 minutes, reducing the liquid by half.

4. Pour the wine into the saucepan and add the peppercorns. Cook 2 minutes, then add the beef stock and return to a boil. Lower the heat and cook another 2–3 minutes. Remove from the heat, cover, and set aside and keep warm.

5. Uncover the elk rack and put it back in the dutch oven. Cook in the barbecue or oven 15–20 minutes, until the meat reaches an internal temperature of 130–140°F for rare/medium-rare. Remove from the oven, cover the meat, and let rest 5 minutes before slicing into chops.

6. Serve 2 chops per person, with a generous spoonful of the apple-peppercorn sauce ladled over each serving.

Elk Stroganoff with Craisin-Portobello Sauce

Do not add salt when you are marinating elk, as it will draw out the moisture of the meat and may prevent even browning.

Serves 6–8

1. Preheat the oven or barbecue to 400°F for indirect heating, putting a water pan under the unheated side of the grill.

2. Season roast with salt and pepper and sear in oil in a dutch oven or roasting pan over medium-high heat, turning to brown all sides.

3. In a small bowl, mix the mushroom soup and onion soup mix, then brush over the roast. Pour steak sauce over the meat and sprinkle chopped onions on top, then place the roast back in the dutch oven and roast 4 hours at 400°F, or until a meat thermometer registers 130°F (rare) or 140°F (medium-rare).

4. Remove the pan and roast from the oven or barbecue, remove the meat and set aside, covered with foil, and let rest while the juices re-circulate.

5. Pour the stock into the pan and stir to incorporate the drippings and scrape up any brown bits in the pan. Add the Craisins, then bring the mixture to a rapid boil.

6. In a small bowl, mix flour and water to form a paste and add slowly to the beef stock, whisking it well to incorporate. When the gravy has thickened, reduce the heat and add the sliced mushrooms. Keep the gravy warm while you slice the meat.

7. Remove the foil from the roast and cut into thin slices. Arrange the meat on a heated platter and drizzle with a small amount of gravy, serving the rest at the table. Garnish with minced parsley, and serve with buttered noodles or roasted or steamed potatoes.

4–5 pound elk roast
1 teaspoon salt
½ teaspoon freshly ground black pepper
¼ cup olive oil
1 (10.5-ounce) can cream of mushroom soup
1 (2-ounce) package onion soup mix
3 tablespoons steak sauce
1 large Spanish onion, chopped
2 cups beef or veal stock
½ cup cherry-flavored Craisins
3 teaspoons flour
2 tablespoons cold water
1 pound portobello mushrooms, sliced
Minced fresh parsley for garnish

Gin-Marinated Elk Back Strap

If you're not a hunter, or don't know one who will give you elk meat, you can order just about any cut online, including roasts, steaks, racks, loins, medallions, sausage, and hamburger and stew meat.

Serves 8–10

Marinade

½ cup minced onion

2–3 grinds black pepper

3 cloves garlic, minced

1 large turnip, peeled and diced

2 stalks celery (including leaves), diced

½ cup shredded carrot

1 cup apple cider or red wine vinegar

1 cup beef stock

1½ cups favorite gin

6–8 pound elk back strap

6–8 slices hickory-smoked bacon

1. In a deep saucepan, combine onion, black pepper, garlic, turnip, celery, carrot, vinegar, and beef stock and bring to a boil over medium-high heat, stirring occasionally. When it reaches a boil, turn heat down to low and simmer 6–8 minutes.

2. Remove the pan from the burner and add the gin, stirring it into the marinade, and let cool.

3. Put the roast into a 2-gallon resealable plastic bag and pour in the cooled marinade. Seal the bag, shake it to distribute the marinade, and refrigerate for at least 48 hours.

4. Remove the meat from the marinade, drain well, reserving marinade, and let the meat come to room temperature. Pour the reserved marinade, including the vegetables, into a deep saucepan and boil 10 minutes. The marinade is now safe to use as a basting liquid.

5. Preheat the barbecue or oven to medium-high (350–400°F) for indirect heating, putting a water pan under the unheated side of the grill. If using an oven, place the water pan on the bottom rack, with the meat on the rack above it.

6. Place the meat on a roasting rack in a dutch oven or large roasting pan and cover it with the bacon, securing it to the roast with toothpicks. Strain out the vegetables and pour the marinade into the roasting pan.

7. Cook in the barbecue or oven for 15 minutes per pound, basting often with the marinade and removing the bacon strips for the last 30 minutes of cooking. Ideally meat should be served rare to medium-rare, 140–150°F.

8. Remove the roast to a warm platter, cover it with aluminum foil, and let rest 5–10 minutes to re-circulate the internal juices before carving.

9. If you wish, whisk 2 tablespoons flour mixed with 2 tablespoons milk into the pan to make a thick, flavorful gravy. You can also add 2–3 tablespoons of gin to the gravy just before serving.

Chicken-Fried Elk Round Steak

You can add grilled onions, crumbled cooked bacon, or golden raisins to the gravy if you wish to add a bit more oomph to the recipe.

Serves 4–6

2 pounds elk round steaks,
    cut into 4-ounce pieces
2 eggs
½ cup milk
1 cup flour
½ teaspoon kosher salt
1 teaspoon freshly ground
    black pepper
1 tablespoon oregano
½ teaspoon paprika
¼ cup butter
2 tablespoons olive oil
2 teaspoons minced parsley
    for garnish

Gravy
¼ cup flour
⅛ teaspoon cayenne pepper
½ teaspoon garlic salt
½ teaspoon onion powder
2 cups skim milk
½ pound small button mushrooms
2 tablespoons minced chives

1. Put the round steaks in a thick plastic resealable bag and tenderize them with a meat mallet, pounding the meat to about ¼ inch thick.

2. In a medium bowl, whisk eggs and milk together. In a wide, deep pan, combine flour, salt, black pepper, oregano, and paprika, stirring to fully incorporate. Dip both sides of the tenderized steaks into the eggs and then dredge both sides in the seasoned flour.

3. Heat butter and olive oil in a cast-iron skillet. Fry the breaded meat over medium-high heat, browning the steaks on both sides until they are golden brown but not overcooked.

4. Remove the cooked steaks from the pan and keep them warm in a 175°F oven. Reserve the drippings in the skillet. If you are cooking the steaks in two batches, pour the drippings from the first batch into a small bowl before you cook the second one. You may have to add more butter and oil to the second batch.

5. To make the gravy, mix the flour, cayenne pepper, salt, onion powder, and milk in a medium bowl. Pour the mixture into the frying pan with all the drippings (adding drippings from first batch if you have them). Stir until the gravy starts to thicken, then add the mushrooms and chives. Continue to stir and cook until the gravy reaches the consistency you like.

6. Remove the steaks from the oven and place on a heated serving platter. Pour the gravy over the steaks and serve, garnished with parsley.

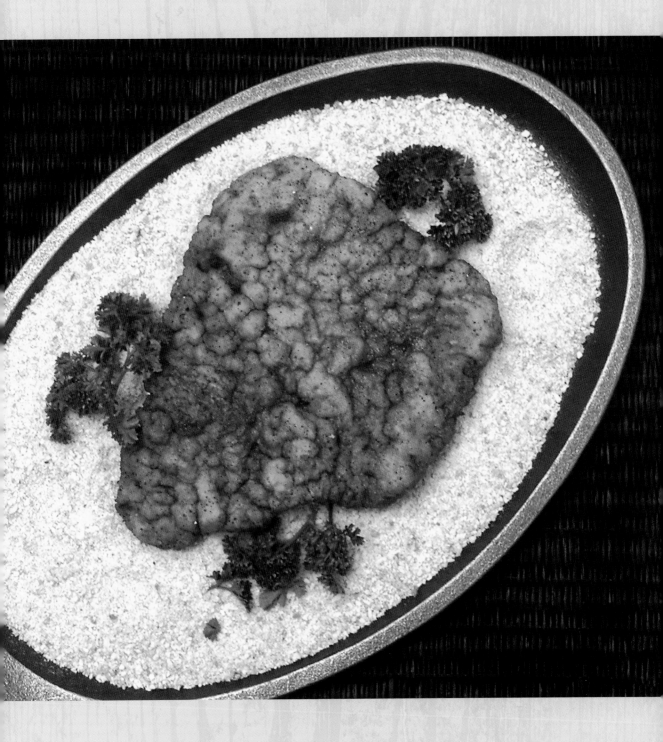

Char-Grilled Elk Tenderloin with Red Miso BBQ Sauce

This recipe was generously shared with us by Chef Jordan Asher, the executive chef at the High Lonesome Ranch in DeBeque, Colorado. He's a dynamic young chef who will be going a long way in the culinary world. The week I spent at the ranch, one of the most spectacular in the country, was a visit to culinary heaven, and combined with the surrounding scenery on the 200-square-mile ranch, one of the best experiences I've ever had outdoors.

Serves 4

Wet Rub

4 cloves garlic, finely chopped
1 tablespoon chopped fresh
    rosemary
1 tablespoon smoked paprika
1 tablespoon chipotle chili powder
1 teaspoon kosher salt
1 teaspoon freshly ground black
    pepper
1 (16-ounce) elk tenderloin
3 tablespoons olive oil

Red Miso BBQ Sauce

1 tablespoon sesame oil
1 tablespoon minced garlic
1 tablespoon minced fresh ginger
1 cup ketchup
2 tablespoons brown sugar
1 ounce cider vinegar
1 tablespoon Worcestershire
    sauce
¼ cup orange juice
1 tablespoon soy sauce
2 ounces red miso
2 tablespoons sliced scallions
    (optional)

1. In a large bowl, combine all the wet rub ingredients and stir. Brush the tenderloin with olive oil, then generously sprinkle the meat with the rub. Cover with plastic wrap and refrigerate 4–8 hours.

2. Remove the meat from the fridge 45 minutes prior to grilling, allowing it come to room temperature.

3. Preheat the barbecue to medium-high (350–400°F).

4. For medium-rare, sear the meat 2 minutes each on all four sides; for medium, add 1 minute per side. Remove the meat from the grill, loosely wrap in aluminum foil, and let rest 5–10 minutes.

5. Heat sesame oil in a small saucepan, then add garlic and ginger and sweat for a few minutes on medium heat. Add the rest of the sauce ingredients and simmer 2 minutes.

6. Remove the sauce from the heat and add the fresh scallions, if using. Slice the tenderloin 1 inch thick in angled cuts (across the grain), place on a heated platter, and drizzle with barbecue sauce.

Elk Cheeseburger Pie

You can make this pie with chunks of meat instead of ground meat, but you must brown the elk with bacon or salt pork first so that it isn't too dry.

Serves 4

1. In a large skillet, heat oil and sauté onions 10–12 minutes over medium-high heat, stirring occasionally. Remove onions with a slotted spoon and set aside.

2. Preheat the oven or barbecue to 350°F.

3. Brown the combined elk and pork in the same pan, about 8–10 minutes. Remove the pan from the heat and drain off as much of the grease as you can. Stir in ketchup, mustard, oregano, and pepper.

4. Unroll the dough from one canister and, using a rolling pin, roll it out on a floured surface to 15 x 15 inches square. Place in a 10 x 10-inch baking dish, so the dough hangs over the edge.

5. Spoon the meat onto the dough, then sprinkle on the cheese, add the onions, and top with the beaten eggs.

6. Roll out the second can of dough the same as the first. Lay the pastry over the top of the baking dish, pressing the top and bottom edges together with a fork dipped in cold water to seal the pie.

7. Cut 3 slits in the pastry to allow steam to escape, then brush the top of the pastry with the egg wash.

8. Place the pie on the middle rack of the oven and bake 35–40 minutes or until the pastry is nicely brown. If the pastry appears to be browning too fast, cover the pie with a loose sheet of aluminum foil.

1 tablespoon extra-virgin olive oil
1 pound white onions, diced
1 pound ground elk
¼ pound ground pork sausage
½ cup ketchup
1 tablespoon prepared yellow mustard
½ teaspoon oregano
½ teaspoon freshly ground black pepper
2 (8-ounce) canisters refrigerated crescent roll dough, room temperature
1½ cups shredded Swiss or cheddar cheese
2 eggs lightly beaten with 1 tablespoon milk

Egg Wash
1 egg yolk beaten with 1 tablespoon water or milk

Elk Jerky

If you don't have a smoker, you can utilize your regular barbecue by banking coals on one side of the barbecue and putting the meat on the grill rack on the unheated side. Directly on top of the coals, place an aluminum foil package of soaked hickory, apple, cherry, or alder chips, with holes punched in the top. You'll need to do this at least 4 or 5 times, reloading sheets of foil each time with fresh, soaked chips to obtain smoke for the time needed to properly smoke the meat.

Serves 8–10

4-pound elk roast

2 tablespoons Worcestershire sauce

1 teaspoon freshly grated ginger

2 teaspoons grated orange zest

2 cups beer

1 cup apple cider vinegar

$1/3$ cup dark soy sauce

$1/4$ cup scotch or whiskey

$1/2$ teaspoon onion powder

2 teaspoons granulated garlic

$1/4$ cup salt

$1/4$ cup brown sugar or whipped honey

1. Trim all visible fat from the roast and cut into $1^{1}/_{2}$- to 2-inch-wide pieces that are about $1/4$ inch thick.

2. Mix the Worcestershire sauce, grated ginger, orange zest, beer, vinegar, soy sauce, scotch, onion powder, garlic, salt, and sugar in a wide glass or ceramic bowl. Pour the marinade into a 2-gallon resealable plastic bag, add the meat strips, shake to distribute, and seal the bag. Marinate 24–36 hours in the refrigerator or a dark, cool place.

3. Remove the meat from the marinade and drain well, discarding the liquid. Place the meat strips on a wire cake rack or grill rack resting in a wide pan (to catch dripping marinade). Let meat sit 45–60 minutes, until it looks somewhat dry and glazed.

4. Preheat the smoker to 150–160°F and smoke meat 12–16 hours, using the foil-wrapped chips throughout the cooking time. Remove to a wire rack and allow to air-dry until glazed, about 45 minutes.

Wild Sheep Chili

Wild sheep meat sometimes has a slightly gamey taste and can be stringy, but the variety of ingredients in this chili and its long cooking time negate both of those qualities.

Serves 4–6

¼ cup olive oil
2 pounds ground sheep meat
    (boneless)
1 (14.5-ounce) can chopped
    tomatoes
1 (15-ounce) can tomato sauce
1 cup red wine
½ cup chopped black olives
½ teaspoon kosher salt
1 tablespoon chili powder
1 teaspoon ground cumin
½ teaspoon ground coriander
1 teaspoon red pepper flakes
1 teaspoon freshly ground
    black pepper
1 cup kidney beans
1 cup black beans
1 cup white beans
Freshly chopped parsley or
    cilantro

Serving Suggestion
Chopped onions
Shredded cheddar cheese
Sour cream

1. In a cast-iron pot or dutch oven over medium-high heat (on a stove top or barbecue side burner), heat the oil until it just begins to smoke, then add the ground sheep meat and brown thoroughly. You may want to do this in 2 or 3 batches so as to not overcrowd the pot and promote even browning. When the meat is browned, remove with a slotted spoon and set aside.

2. Add tomatoes, tomato sauce, wine, olives, salt, chili powder, cumin, coriander, red pepper flakes, and black pepper, and stir. Bring to a boil, then reduce the heat to a simmer, cover the pot, and cook 3 hours, stirring occasionally. Then add in the beans and cook for 30–45 minutes.

3. Bring to a boil, add meat, then reduce the heat to a simmer, cover the pot, and cook for 3½–4 hours, stirring occasionally.

4. When the meat is fork tender, and the beans soft, remove the pot from the heat, sprinkle chopped parsley or cilantro on top, and serve chili immediately. Provide chopped onions, shredded cheddar cheese, and a bowl of sour cream for people to add to the chili, and serve with garlic or corn bread on the side.

Butterflied Leg of Rocky Mountain Sheep

Mountain sheep is a game meat prized for its tenderness and sweetness. The meat has a bit more fat marbled throughout it compared to other wild game of this sort. You can treat it like lamb in most dishes.

Serves 8–10

Mint Sauce
1 cup white vinegar
¼ cup granulated sugar
1 cup finely chopped fresh mint
   leaves

Marinade
2 medium onions, coarsely
   chopped
5 cloves garlic
3 tablespoons chopped fresh
   rosemary
Zest of 1 lemon
Zest of 1 lime
1 tablespoon red wine vinegar
2 tablespoons pomegranate
   balsamic vinegar
1 cup red wine, divided
3 tablespoons extra-virgin olive oil

6–7 pound sheep leg, boned and
   butterflied
1 teaspoon seasoned salt
1 teaspoon freshly ground black
   pepper

1. In a small saucepan over medium-high heat, combine vinegar and sugar for mint sauce, stirring until the sugar is dissolved. Bring just to a boil and then remove from heat.

2. Add mint leaves and stir well. Let the mixture sit until the mint leaves have flavored the sauce to your satisfaction. Strain the mint leaves out and discard. Store the cooled sauce in a covered container until needed.

3. To make the marinade, put the onions, garlic, rosemary, lemon and lime zests, vinegars, ½ cup of the wine, and olive oil into a food processor and pulse until it becomes a thick paste.

4. Season the butterflied leg with salt and pepper and put into a 2-gallon resealable bag. Add the marinade and shake and roll the bag to spread it all over the meat. Seal the bag and refrigerate overnight, turning the bag several times.

5. Remove the meat from the bag, wipe off excess marinade, reserve it, and let the leg come to room temperature, about 30 minutes.

6. Preheat the barbecue to medium (300–350°F) for indirect heating, putting a water pan under the unheated side of the grill.

7. Pour the marinade into a saucepan, add the second ½ cup of wine, and boil at least 10 minutes. Cool and set aside.

8. Place the butterflied leg on a well-oiled grill over the direct heat and cook about 5 minutes per side to sear the meat, then move to the unheated side of the grill and cook approximately 45–60 minutes, turning the meat several times. The sheep is done when a thermometer inserted into the thick part of the meat reads 130°F (for medium-rare).

9. Place the meat on a cutting board, wrap it well with aluminum foil, and let it rest 10–15 minutes to let the juices recirculate.

10. Remove the foil and cut the meat (across the grain of, course) into ¼- to ½-inch-thick slices. Serve with the mint sauce.

Mountain Goat Curry

For a tropical touch, stir in a 15-ounce can of coconut milk the last ten minutes of cooking.

Serves 4

3 pounds goat meat, taken from
    bone-in leg
1 teaspoon kosher salt
3 tablespoons olive or corn oil
2 tablespoons curry powder,
    divided
1 large white or yellow onion,
    diced
3 cloves garlic, minced
Juice of 2 limes
1 small Scotch bonnet pepper,
    seeded and finely minced
1 teaspoon chopped fresh thyme
1 teaspoon marjoram
1 bunch green onions, cut into
    green and white parts,
    chopped
1 teaspoon fresh chopped
    rosemary
1 teaspoon seasoning salt
½ teaspoon black pepper
Water
5 medium potatoes, quartered

1. Wash, pat dry, and season meat with kosher salt.

2. In a dutch oven or roasting pan, heat oil and add 1 tablespoon curry powder. Cook while stirring constantly until the curry powder darkens, about 2–3 minutes, but don't burn it.

3. Add meat to the dutch oven, along with onion, garlic, lime juice, and Scotch bonnet, and sauté about 4 minutes over medium heat.

4. Add thyme, marjoram, green onions, rosemary, 1 tablespoon curry powder, seasoning salt, and black pepper. Cover with water and simmer, uncovered, until meat is very tender and sauce is thick, about 2–2½ hours. Add more water if necessary.

5. Add quartered potatoes to the pot during last 20 minutes of cooking and simmer, covered, until potatoes are fork tender.

6. Serve with grilled or steamed corn on the cob, or grilled vegetables like carrots, eggplant, zucchini, and asparagus.

Goat Teriyaki with Mushrooms

You can, of course, buy commercial teriyaki sauce, but it's so easy to make, plus you can add flavors or change ingredients at will. The basics: soy sauce, ginger, garlic, green onions, and brown sugar.

Serves 6

2½–3 pounds leg of goat
1 cup dark soy sauce
1 cup rice wine
3 tablespoons freshly grated
    ginger
6 cloves garlic, minced
1 bunch green onions, green and
    white parts, chopped
½ cup brown sugar
16 ounces whole mushrooms
4 large onions, quartered
    and divided
¼ cup olive oil

1. Cut the meat into 2-inch cubes, remove any excess fat, and place the meat in a 2-gallon resealable plastic bag.

2. In a medium bowl, mix soy sauce, wine, ginger, garlic, green onions, and brown sugar. Pour into the plastic bag over the goat meat chunks, seal the bag, and marinate overnight in the refrigerator.

3. Remove the meat from the marinade. Pour the marinade into a saucepan and boil for 10 minutes while the goat comes to room temperature. Preheat the barbecue to medium-high (350–400°F).

4. Thread the meat on metal skewers, alternating with whole mushrooms and 2- or 3-layer sections of the onions. Brush with olive oil and cook over direct flames or coals 3–4 minutes per side, brushing with the reheated marinade and turning several times to brown all the meat.

5. Serve with couscous or cooked rice.

Grilled Moose *au Chocolat*

Actually, this is a molé dish combining a traditional Mexican poblano mole sauce, which is made with chocolate, with seared and grilled moose steaks . . . hence moose *au chocolat*!

Serves 4

¼ cup butter

¼ cup olive oil

4 moose steaks

¼ cup plus 2 tablespoons flour, divided

¼ cup honey

½ teaspoon seasoned salt

¼ teaspoon freshly ground black pepper

Chocolate Mole Sauce

4 dried poblano chilies, stems and seeds removed

4 dried New Mexican red chilies, stems and seeds removed

1 medium onion, chopped

2 cloves garlic, chopped

2 medium tomatoes, peeled and seeds removed, chopped

2 tablespoons sesame seeds, divided

½ cup almonds

½ corn tortilla, torn into pieces (optional)

¼ cup raisins

¼ teaspoon ground cloves

¼ teaspoon ground cinnamon

¼ teaspoon ground coriander

3 tablespoons shortening or vegetable oil

1 cup chicken broth

2 wedges (about 0.4 ounce each) Ibarra Mexican bitter chocolate (or more to taste)

Sour cream

1. Preheat barbecue or oven to 300°F.

2. Melt butter in a large frying pan and add olive oil. Dredge moose steaks in ¼ cup flour and brown them on both sides over high heat, approximately 3 minutes per side. Drain the steaks, discarding the oil.

3. Place the browned moose steaks in a cast-iron skillet or dutch oven.

4. In a small bowl or measuring cup, mix honey, salt, and pepper and pour the mixture over the top of the moose steaks.

5. Roast the moose steaks, covered, in the barbecue or oven or barbecue grill until tender, about 2 hours. When cooked, leave in oven with heat turned off to keep warm.

6. While steaks are cooking, make the mole by pureeing the chilies, onion, garlic, tomatoes, 1 tablespoon sesame seeds, almonds, tortilla pieces (optional), raisins, cloves, cinnamon, coriander, and 2 tablespoons flour in a blender until smooth.

7. Melt shortening in a skillet and sauté the puree for 10 minutes, stirring frequently. Add chicken broth and chocolate and cook over very low heat for 45 minutes. The sauce should be very thick.

8. Pour the sauce into 4 stemmed dessert glasses and top with a dollop of sour cream, to make the sauce look like mousse (moose) *au chocolat*. Serve a steak, garnished with the remaining sesame seeds, and a "dessert" glass to each guest.

Note: Ibarra chocolate is available in the Mexican foods aisle of larger supermarkets. It also makes wonderful hot chocolate. If you can't find Ibarra chocolate, substitute 1 ounce semi-sweet chocolate or 1 tablespoon semi-sweet cocoa powder plus 1/2 teaspoon ground cinnamon for the two wedges called for in this recipe.

Apple-Prune-Stuffed Moose Chops

Henry David Thoreau was a huge fan of moose meat, writing in *The Maine Woods* that moose meat is "like tender beef, with perhaps more flavor; sometimes like veal." While I might disagree with favorably comparing dark meat moose with white meat veal, certainly the taste is more like tender beef than "game." In this recipe, adding the fruit gives an extra bit of sweet to the fairly dense meat.

Serves 6

6 moose chops, cut 1½ inches thick
1½ cups favorite stuffing mix
¼ cup chopped apples
¼ cup chopped prunes
½ cup shredded extra-sharp
   cheddar cheese
2 tablespoons butter, melted
2 tablespoons apple or prune juice
¼ teaspoon kosher salt
¼ teaspoon garlic powder
⅛ teaspoon nutmeg
Favorite barbecue sauce

1. Preheat the oven or barbecue to 350°F.

2. Cut a pocket in the side of each moose chop.

3. In a large bowl, combine stuffing mix, apples, prunes, and cheese. In another bowl, combine melted butter, apple or prune juice, salt, garlic, and nutmeg. Stir the butter mixture into the stuffing mixture until well blended.

4. Lightly stuff the moose chops with the buttered stuffing. Seal the edges with toothpicks so stuffing doesn't leak out.

5. Place the stuffed chops in a shallow roasting pan or cast-iron skillet and bake, uncovered, 1 hour.

6. Drizzle each chop with 1–2 tablespoons barbecue sauce, cover with foil, and cook another 15 minutes.

7. Serve with mashed potatoes and corn on the cob.

Swedish Moose Tenderloin

Moose are found in huge numbers in Sweden, Finland, Norway, and Poland, in addition to some northern and western United States, the Canadian Rockies, and Canada's Maritime Provinces, and more! You don't have to get a Swedish moose for this recipe—any old domestic moose will do.

Serves 3–4

1. Preheat the grill or oven to 400°F.

2. Rub the olive oil into the tenderloin, then lightly salt and pepper. Sear both sides of the tenderloin in a cast-iron or ovenproof skillet until the meat is well marked.

3. Move the meat to the indirect or unheated side of the grill and cook about 30–35 minutes, until a meat thermometer inserted in the roast reads 150°F. Remove meat from heat, seal it in foil, and let rest 10 minutes. The temperature will rise to 155–160°F during that time.

4. While tenderloin is cooking, sauté the shallots and mushrooms in the olive oil in a saucepan. Pour in the wine and stock and reduce until about a quarter is left. Whip in the butter and add salt and pepper to taste. Add parsley and chives right before serving.

5. Drizzle tenderloin slices with some sauce, reserving the remaining sauce to serve at the table. Serve with garlic mashed potatoes and freshly steamed broccoli or brussels sprouts.

1½ pounds moose tenderloin
2 tablespoons olive oil
½ teaspoon kosher salt
Freshly ground black pepper

Sauce
2 large shallots, chopped
7 ounces fresh button or crimini mushrooms, coarsely chopped
¼ cup olive oil
1⅔ cups red wine
3½ cups beef or veal stock
¼ cup cold butter
2 teaspoons kosher salt
1 teaspoon freshly ground black pepper
1 tablespoon freshly chopped parsley
1 tablespoon minced chives

Bullwinkle's Stroganoff

Since moose, like most wild game meats, is very lean, we use bacon and bacon fat in this recipe to keep the meat moist. You can forgo the bacon fat and use olive oil, but you'll lose a lot of taste.

Serves 4

1½ pounds moose sirloin steak, cut into ½-inch strips

¼ cup plus 2 tablespoons flour, divided

1 teaspoon garlic salt

1 clove garlic, minced

2 strips bacon, diced

½ cup chopped porcini mushrooms

½ cup chopped onions

2 tablespoons bacon fat or olive oil

1 tablespoon Worcestershire sauce

1 cup beef stock (low sodium)

1 cup sour cream

Serving Suggestion
Cooked, buttered noodles or wild rice

1. Dredge the steak strips in ¼ cup flour and salt.

2. Sauté garlic, bacon, mushrooms, and onions in fat over medium heat for 5 minutes; add meat and brown. Remove meat, bacon, mushrooms, and onions from the pan.

3. Add the remaining 2 tablespoons flour to drippings in pan and stir. Add Worcestershire sauce and beef stock and cook until thickened, about 5 minutes, stirring often. Add sour cream and heat until gravy just begins to boil.

4. Turn down the heat, add the cooked moose and vegetables, and heat 3 more minutes.

5. Ladle stroganoff over cooked and buttered noodles or wild rice.

Gravenhurst Moose Chili

This recipe comes to you all the way from Gravenhurst, Ontario, Canada, near Lake Muskoka. It was there where I first tasted moose chili as a child, and I've never forgotten that first bowl. This is an updated and slightly altered version of a very old recipe—Grandma would never have used beer.

Serves 10–12

1. In a deep stockpot or large dutch oven, melt bacon fat over medium heat and sauté onions, garlic, and jalapeños until tender, about 20 minutes.

2. Add moose meat and the salts and cook 20 minutes. Add canned chipotle, the chili powders, cumin, oregano, and basil and cook 5 minutes, stirring frequently.

3. Add tomatoes, sugar, stock, and beer and bring to a boil. Reduce the heat to low, cover the pot, and simmer 2–2½ hours, stirring occasionally. Add the cooked beans and continue simmering until the beans are just warmed through, stirring to blend well.

4. Provide bowls of sour cream, chopped onions, and shredded cheese for your guests to add to their chili. Serve with thick slices of garlic bread on the side.

¼ cup bacon fat
2 large onions, chopped
8 cloves garlic, minced
4 medium fresh jalapeños, minced
3 pounds moose meat, chili grind
1 teaspoon kosher salt
1 teaspoon garlic salt
1 (7-ounce) can Herdez (or other brand) chipotle chilies in adobo sauce
½ cup chili powder
3 tablespoons ancho chili powder
2 tablespoons ground cumin
2 tablespoons dried oregano
1 teaspoon dried basil
1 (14.5-ounce) can chopped tomatoes
¼ cup brown sugar
4 cups beef stock
24 ounces beer
4 cups cooked black beans
4 cups cooked pinto beans

Serving Suggestion
1 cup sour cream
Finely chopped onion
1 cup shredded cheddar cheese

Presque Isle Moose Pot Roast

Unfortunately, you cannot buy moose meat in the United States, so your only source is to bring home a moose yourself, or find a hunter who has bagged one of North America's biggest creatures and is willing to share some of its tasty meat.

Serves 4–6

4 pounds moose roast

¼ cup cubed bacon

2 tablespoons olive oil

1½ cups favorite red wine (I like either pinot noir or merlot.)

1 cup apple cider or Cran-Apple juice

2 stalks celery, chopped

1 teaspoon freshly chopped parsley

¼ teaspoon oregano

¼ teaspoon minced fresh basil

3 cloves garlic, minced

1 (6-ounce) can tomato paste

1 teaspoon kosher salt

1 teaspoon freshly ground black pepper

8 new potatoes, cubed with skin on

6 carrots, cubed

6 medium yellow or white onions, chopped

3 tablespoons butter

2–3 tablespoons flour (to thicken gravy)

4–5 fresh parsley sprigs for garnish

1. Using a sharp knife, cut small slits in the roast and insert pieces of bacon into them.

2. Heat olive oil in a dutch oven or deep cast-iron pot and brown the roast on all sides.

3. Add wine, fruit juice, celery, parsley, oregano, basil, garlic, tomato paste, salt, and pepper. Cover and simmer gently 3 hours on top of the stove, or in the oven or barbecue at 350°F, until the meat is tender. If liquid gets low, add water or more fruit juice.

4. About 1 hour before the meal is to be served, add potatoes, carrots, onions, and butter, and stir. When vegetables are tender, remove them along with the meat and place in a covered container to keep warm.

5. Thicken the gravy with flour, whisking it into the liquid 1 tablespoon at a time until it coats the back of a spoon.

6. Slice the roast and place on a large platter, surrounding the meat with the vegetables. Pour the gravy over everything and serve, garnished with fresh parsley sprigs.

Venison Loin Chops with Mango Chutney

As with most wild game, prompt and correct field dressing is vital to obtaining the best-tasting meat. The animal should be dressed and cooled as soon as possible to bring down the internal temperature and ensure safe, tasty meat.

Serves 4

Chutney

4 medium peaches, peeled, stones removed, and coarsely chopped

3 medium mangos, peeled and coarsely chopped

1 cup sugar

2 cups white wine vinegar

1 teaspoon cardamom

1 teaspoon ground ginger

1 teaspoon salt

1 teaspoon white pepper

1 red bell pepper, finely diced

1 cup golden raisins

½ red onion, finely diced

Baste

½ cup olive oil

2 cloves garlic, chopped and lightly browned

1 sprig rosemary

1 sprig thyme

2 teaspoons black peppercorns

8-bone venison loin roast

1 tablespoon olive oil

½ teaspoon kosher salt

Freshly ground black pepper

4 (¼-inch) slices sweet potato, grilled

4 (¼-inch) slices white potato, grilled

1. Combine all the chutney ingredients in a saucepan and simmer, uncovered, 45 minutes. Cool, then place in a clean jar and refrigerate. Warm before serving. Preheat barbecue to 350°F.

2. Combine all the baste ingredients in a small bowl.

3. Brush loin with oil, then generously salt and pepper the roast. Place on a heated grill and cook 4–5 minutes per side, until meat is cooked the way you like it, basting every time you turn meat. Let loin rest 5 minutes, then slice into chops for serving.

4. Place the venison chops on top of grilled sweet potato and white potato slices and sprinkle with fresh rosemary. Serve with the chutney available on the side.

Garlic-Pepper Venison Tenderloin

If venison is overcooked (beyond 140–150°F), it quickly becomes dry and tough, so please cook only to rare or medium-rare.

Serves 4–5

1 tablespoon granulated garlic

2 teaspoons kosher salt

2 tablespoons freshly ground
  black pepper

¼ teaspoon red pepper flakes

2 tablespoons plus 2 teaspoons
  olive oil, divided

2-pound venison fillet

1 teaspoon butter

1. Preheat the barbecue or oven to medium-high (350–400°F) for indirect heating, putting a water pan under the unheated side of the grill.

2. In a flat pan, mix garlic, salt, black pepper, and red pepper flakes. Rub 2 tablespoons olive oil into the fillet, working it well into all surfaces.

3. Roll the tenderloin in the spice mix, pressing down to coat all sides (including the ends) of the meat with the spices.

4. In a large heavy skillet, heat the remaining 2 teaspoons olive oil with the butter, and sear the meat quickly over high heat.

5. Place the skillet in the barbecue or oven and roast the meat 10–12 minutes or until rare to medium-rare (130–140°F).

6. Slice and serve with skillet corn and baked potatoes.

Venison-Stuffed Bell Peppers

These stuffed peppers can also be made with ground bear, elk, moose, or even wild boar, or a mixture of several game meats.

Serves 4-5

1 large onion, diced
2 tablespoons olive oil
1 tablespoon minced garlic
1 tablespoon balsamic vinegar
1 teaspoon oregano
1 teaspoon chopped fresh basil
1 teaspoon celery salt
½ teaspoon black pepper
½ cup diced fresh mushrooms
1 (16-ounce) can corn kernels, drained
1 pound ground venison
2 tablespoons olive oil
1 cup stuffing cubes
4–5 large bell peppers (red, green, or yellow)
1 (16-ounce) can tomato sauce
1 (16-ounce) can chopped tomatoes
1 cup water or red wine

1. Preheat the oven or barbecue to medium-high (350–400°F).

2. In a cast-iron skillet, cook onions in oil until translucent. Add garlic, vinegar, spices, mushrooms, and corn and heat through.

3. In another saucepan, sauté ground venison in olive oil. When browned, drain off grease. Add stuffing cubes and stir well. Pour the mixture into the skillet with the mushrooms and corn and stir to thoroughly mix.

4. Cut off the top ¼ to ½ inch of the peppers, remove the seeds and membrane, and fill the peppers with the meat filling, packing lightly so the peppers are well filled.

5. In a dutch oven or deep roasting pan, combine tomato sauce, chopped tomatoes, and water or wine and stir. Liquid should cover the bottom of the pan by 1 to 1½ inches; add more water or wine if you are a bit shy of this measurement.

6. Place the peppers open end up in a dutch oven. Cook in the oven or barbecue 25–30 minutes or until peppers are just beginning to get tender.

7. Remove the peppers to a platter. Pour the sauce into a sauceboat and serve at the table with the peppers.

Grilled Loin of Venison with Wild Mushrooms

Like most large game, the fat of venison can be very strongly flavored, so it should be removed and the meat cooked with cream, lard, butter, or cooking oil to keep it moist.

Serves 4–6

2 ½–3-pound loin of venison

Marinade
1 cup red wine
2 tablespoons olive oil
2 tablespoons soy sauce
1 teaspoon garlic powder
1 teaspoon tarragon
Juice of 1 lemon
½ teaspoon black pepper

8–10 strips bacon, cut in 2-inch
   lengths

Wine Baste
1 cup red wine
½ cup olive oil
1 tablespoon balsamic vinegar

Mushroom Ragout
3 pounds fresh wild mushrooms
   (shiitake, chanterelle, oyster,
   morel, and straw varieties),
   mixed and chopped
1 medium onion, chopped
½ cup butter
2 tablespoons olive oil
¾ cup red wine
Juice of ½ lemon
Pinch of marjoram

1. Prepare the loin by removing the white shiny muscle sheath on the outside of the meat and cutting a ½-inch slit the full length of loin.

2. Whisk together the marinade ingredients. Put the loin in a resealable plastic bag and cover with marinade; store overnight in the refrigerator.

3. Remove the meat from the marinade, drain well, and allow it to come to room temperature, resting covered for 10 minutes. Boil the remaining marinade for 10 minutes so you can use as a basting liquid.

4. Prepare the barbecue to 250–300°F for indirect heat, with a water pan under the area of the grill where the meat will be placed. Fit bacon strips in the long slit you cut into the loin, and cook the meat to desired doneness (like prime rib, the rarer the better). Baste the loin with the wine baste occasionally. The meat should take 30–40 minutes in the barbecue or oven and reach an internal temperature of 160°F.

5. While the meat is cooking, sauté the mushroom ragout ingredients in a large cast-iron skillet until most of the liquid evaporates.

6. Remove the meat from the oven and serve on a bed of the mushroom ragout. Garnish with fresh sprigs of rosemary and marjoram.

Black Buck's Venison Chili

Venison is lower in calories, cholesterol, and fat than most cuts of beef, lamb, or pork and is now being recommended by nutritionists to people who are trying to lose weight or need to adhere to a low-fat diet.

Serves 4–6

4 pounds boneless venison, cubed
¼ cup bacon grease
2 onions, chopped
2 fresh jalapeños, seeded and and chopped
½ cup chopped green bell pepper
½ cup chopped red bell pepper
2 cloves garlic, chopped
12 ounces favorite beer
1 ounce whiskey
½ teaspoon cayenne pepper
3 tablespoons Worcestershire sauce
⅓ cup ground cumin
⅓ cup chili powder
½ teaspoon salt
2 tablespoons cornmeal
2 (16-ounce) cans stewed tomatoes
1 (8-ounce) can tomato sauce
1 cup red wine

Serving Suggestion
Grilled red pepper caps
Chopped onions
Shredded cheddar cheese
Sour cream

1. In a dutch oven or deep roasting pan, brown venison in bacon grease. Remove the meat and set aside.

2. In the remaining grease, sauté onions, jalapeños, bell peppers, and garlic until onions start to become transparent. Add beer, whiskey, cayenne, Worcestershire sauce, cumin, chili powder, and salt to onions and peppers, along with the browned meat. Boil gently for 5–7 minutes.

3. Reduce the heat to medium and add cornmeal, stewed tomatoes, tomato sauce, and wine, stirring occasionally while continuing to cook for 30 minutes.

4. Reduce the heat to a simmer and cook 1 hour, stirring occasionally.

5. Serve with grilled red pepper caps, chopped onions, shredded cheddar cheese, sour cream, and chilled mugs of very cold beer.

Devil's Thumb Venison Stew

This recipe is based on one shared with us by Executive Chef Ken Ohlinger, who heads up the dining programs at the award-winning Devil's Thumb Ranch, an eco-friendly year-round ranch resort, spa, and corporate retreat in Colorado.

Serves 4

1 pound venison stew meat
Flour for dredging
1 teaspoon kosher salt
1 teaspoon freshly ground black
  pepper
4 tablespoons vegetable oil
1 cup sliced shiitake mushroom
  caps
½ cup caramelized onions
1 cup red wine
2 quarts venison, beef, or veal
  stock
4 (5-ounce) venison loin
  medallions
3 cups parsnip puree (16 peeled
  parsnips boiled in cream,
  strained, and pureed)

Serving Suggestion
1 cantaloupe, seeded and cut into
  1-inch-thick half moons
¼ cup honey

1. Preheat the oven to 350°F.

2. Lightly flour and season venison stew meat with salt and pepper. In a sauté pan or skillet with a lid, brown the stew meat in vegetable oil.

3. Once browned, remove the meat and add sliced shiitake mushrooms and caramelized onions. Once fully sweated, add stew meat back to the pan and add red wine. Reduce by half.

4. Add stock, place in the oven, and cook until meat is tender, about 2–2½ hours.

5. After the stew meat is cooked, sear the venison loin medallions over high heat in a sauté pan. Once seared on all sides, place in the oven for 5–7 minutes for a medium-rare loin.

6. Rest the loin medallions for 5 minutes before slicing. Warm up parsnip puree, and place one quarter on each plate. Form a well in the center of the puree. Spoon a heavy amount of the stew in the center of the well, and place the sliced loin over the top of stew.

7. Serve with grilled cantaloupe brushed with honey and generously seasoned with freshly ground black pepper, and a very cold beer.

Betty's Venison Enchiladas

Beraselda "Betty" Garcia is the delightful cook at the High Lonesome Ranch in McMullen County, Texas. She is one of the best pure cooks I have ever met, and her cooking, combined with the charm of the Lonesome Dove village at this ranch, provided me a wonderful fishing, hunting, and eating experience. She gleefully shared this recipe with me.

Serves 4–6

2 tablespoons olive oil
2 pounds venison stew meat
1 cup smoky barbecue sauce
1 large onion, chopped
2 large tomatoes, chopped
2 tablespoons chili powder
1 large fresh jalapeño, finely
   chopped
1 tablespoon freshly minced garlic
1 teaspoon kosher salt
½ teaspoon freshly ground
   black pepper
2 cans red enchilada sauce (La
   Victoria or El Pato brands)
8–12 flour tortillas
3 cups *queso fresco* Mexican
   cheese

1. Preheat the oven or barbecue to high heat (400°F).

2. In a heavy cast-iron skillet over high heat, brown venison and onions in olive oil.

3. When the meat is browned, add barbecue sauce, tomatoes, chili powder, jalapeño, garlic, salt, and pepper and cook 5 minutes. Add enchilada sauce and stir well; cover and simmer 30 minutes.

4. Spray the bottom of a large frying pan with nonstick cooking or grilling spray. Over medium heat, warm each tortilla in the pan until it becomes soft. Set the softened tortillas aside, covered with a warm, moist towel.

5. Fill tortillas with a generous 2–3 tablespoons of the meat mixture and 1 tablespoon *queso fresco,* then roll and place them in a casserole dish, side by side, seam down until the dish is filled.

6. Ladle the remaining meat mixture over the enchiladas. Cover with the remaining cheese and bake until the cheese is melted and starts to brown, about 8–10 minutes.

7. Serve with Mexican rice and freshly made pico de gallo.

Tangy Venison Meat Loaf

Since venison is leaner than other red meats, ground pork has been added to this recipe for extra richness. Serve as a main course or in small slices, chilled, as an appetizer.

Serves 8

1 large onion, finely chopped
1 carrot, finely minced
1 tablespoon vegetable oil
1½ pounds ground venison
¾ pound ground pork
½ cup panko bread crumbs
⅓ cup milk (or, for a richer loaf, half-and-half)
1 teaspoon kosher salt
¾ teaspoon sage
½ teaspoon oregano
½ teaspoon ground cumin
¼ teaspoon freshly ground black pepper
¾ cup sour plum jam, divided
2 tablespoons whiskey or scotch
1 large egg, lightly beaten
1 tablespoon lemon juice
Minced fresh parsley for garnish

1. Preheat the oven or barbecue to 350°F. Lightly grease or spray a 9 x 5 x 3-inch loaf pan; set aside.

2. In a large cast-iron skillet, sauté onion and carrot in vegetable oil until soft, about 6–8 minutes. Transfer to a bowl and cool.

3. Stir in venison, ground pork, panko, milk, salt, sage, oregano, cumin, pepper, ½ cup of the jam, whiskey, and beaten egg and mix well. Spoon the meat into the prepared loaf pan, tamp down to remove air pockets, smooth the top with a spoon, and cover with aluminum foil.

4. Bake 50–60 minutes or until the meat loaf is firm and cooked through—the temperature inside should be 160°F. Cool in the pan for 10 minutes, drain off any grease, and invert the loaf onto a serving platter.

5. Mix the remaining plum jam with the lemon juice and spread on top of the meat loaf. Sprinkle with parsley and serve immediately.

Venison Burgers

Venison meat, like most wild game, needs some help in keeping moist and juicy when cooked. We're adding ground pork and bacon here, but you could also use pork sausage, pork belly, or another fatty meat to supplement the drier game meat.

Serves 6–8

6 slices bacon, minced
2 tablespoons olive oil
1 teaspoon minced garlic
2 large shallots, minced
2 pounds ground venison
¼ pound ground pork
1 tablespoon Worcestershire sauce
1 tablespoon chopped fresh parsley
½ teaspoon hickory-smoked salt
Freshly ground black pepper
1 egg, beaten

1. Cook bacon in a skillet over medium heat until browned and crispy. Pour bacon and 1 tablespoon of the bacon grease into a heatproof bowl and allow to cool.

2. Heat olive oil in another skillet and add garlic and shallots; stir and cook until softened, about 3 minutes. Add to the bowl of bacon and grease, and stir in venison, pork, Worcestershire sauce, parsley, salt, a couple generous grinds of black pepper, and the beaten egg.

3. Cover the bowl and refrigerate the meat 20–25 minutes.

4. Preheat the barbecue to medium-high (350–400°F), making sure the grill is well oiled or sprayed.

5. Shape meat into 6–8 patties and grill to your desired doneness. Serve on buttered and toasted hamburger buns or focaccia bread, accompanied by your favorite condiments.

Venison BBQ Pot Roast

You could also use turnips, brussels sprouts, or white, red, Yukon Gold, or sweet potatoes in place of the carrots and parsnips in this recipe.

Serves 6–8

1. Preheat the barbecue or oven to 350°F.

2. Roll the roast in flour and season with onion salt and pepper.

3. Brown the roast in olive oil in a large roasting pan over medium-high heat. When nicely brown all over, add the onion slices, pineapple, beef broth, tomatoes, carrots, parsnips, oregano, and garlic powder. Cover and place in the barbecue or oven.

4. Cook 3–4 hours, ladling gravy over the roast occasionally, until the meat is fork tender.

3-pound venison roast
¼ cup flour
1 teaspoon onion salt
Freshly ground black pepper
2 tablespoons olive oil
2 large onions, sliced
½ cup pineapple chunks, drained
2 cups beef broth
1 (14.5-ounce) can chopped
    tomatoes
1 cup chopped carrots
1 cup chopped parsnips
2 teaspoons oregano
2 teaspoons garlic powder

Texas Boar Medallions with Raspberry Gravy

You can easily make your own raspberry vinegar by mixing a 16-ounce bottle of white wine vinegar with a cup of fresh raspberries in a large glass bottle. Tightly cover it and let sit in a cool, dark place for a couple weeks before using.

Serves 4–6

3 pounds boar tenderloin, sliced
    into 6-ounce medallions
2 cups flour
1 teaspoon garlic powder
1 teaspoon rosemary
1 teaspoon savory
1 teaspoon celery salt
½ cup olive oil
1 pint button mushrooms,
    with stems removed
1½ quarts chicken stock
⅓ cup raspberry vinegar
¼ cup unsalted butter
¼ cup finely chopped parsley
½ teaspoon salt
¼ teaspoon freshly ground
    black pepper
1 pint raspberries

1. Pound the boar medallions until they are very thin, then set aside.

2. In a wide, flat bowl, mix flour, garlic powder, rosemary, savory, and celery salt. Dredge the medallions in the seasoned flour.

3. In a hot skillet over medium heat, sauté the boar medallions in olive oil until they are brown on both sides, then remove them from the pan to a heated platter. Cover the meat with aluminum foil and place in an oven or barbecue (off the heat) at 200°F to keep warm.

4. Add the mushroom caps to the grease remaining in the pan (you may need to add 1–2 tablespoons more olive oil) and cook until they are brown and softened. Remove the mushrooms from the pan and place in a covered bowl next to the meat in the oven.

5. Deglaze the pan by adding stock and stirring up the browned bits from the bottom of the pan. Add the raspberry vinegar, turn the heat to high, and simmer, reducing the liquid by half. When reduced, add butter, parsley, salt, and pepper, and whisk until well mixed. Gently fold the raspberries into the warm gravy and set aside while you remove the cooked medallions from the oven.

6. Place 1 or 2 medallions on each plate, divide the mushrooms equally over the meat, pour on the raspberry gravy, and serve immediately.

Wild Boar in Chocolate

Wild boar meat is darker and the grain is tighter than domestic pork, and it has "soft" fat compared to the "hard" fat of its domestic relatives. As with all fat, the excess should be trimmed off the meat before you cook it.
Serves 8–10

5-pound wild boar roast

1 (25.4-ounce) bottle red wine

2 yellow onions, diced, divided

¼ cup olive oil

2 carrots, chopped

2 stalks celery, chopped

1 heaping tablespoon juniper berries

1 teaspoon kosher salt

1 teaspoon freshly ground black pepper

1 cup chopped dried apricots

½ cup sugar

1 tablespoon freshly minced garlic

½ cup red wine vinegar, room temperature

½ cup grated Ibarra Mexican chocolate

1 cup chopped dried prunes, chopped

1 cup cream sherry (not "cooking" sherry)

1. Place the meat in a large resealable plastic bag and add the wine and half of the chopped onions. Seal the bag and refrigerate overnight, turning the bag occasionally to distribute the marinade.

2. With a slotted spoon, remove the meat and dry with paper towels, reserve marinade. Preheat the oven or barbecue to 250°F.

3. In a large dutch oven, brown the meat in olive oil over high heat. Pour the wine and onion marinade over the meat and add carrots, celery, remaining onions, juniper berries, salt, and pepper. Cook in the oven or barbecue for 3 hours or until tender.

4. Allow the meat to cool in the cooking liquid, skimming off fat that forms on the surface, then remove and cut the cooled meat into 1½- to 2-inch chunks, discarding the bone. Strain the marinade and pour the remaining liquid back into the dutch oven with the meat.

5. Soak the chopped apricots in warm water until plumped, about 15 minutes, then drain and set aside.

6. In a small saucepan over medium-high, heat sugar in 2 tablespoons water until it caramelizes and turns light brown, then stir in garlic. Add vinegar and grated chocolate and boil 2 minutes, then add plumped apricots, prunes, and cream sherry to the sauce.

7. Pour the sauce over the meat in the dutch oven and simmer 10 minutes either on the stovetop or back in the oven.

8. Remove the meat and arrange on a platter, then pour the sauce over the meat and serve. This dish goes very well with steamed Thai jasmine rice.

Kate's Wild Boar Feta Burgers

Instead of feta, you could try a strong-flavored cheese like Huntsman (a combination of Stilton and Double Gloucester) or, for those who like a milder flavor, a French Brie like Brie de Meaux, probably the best of that breed.

Serves 4

1. Preheat the barbecue to medium-high (350–400°F).

2. Place ground boar meat, feta, shallots, pesto, and black pepper in a medium bowl and mix until just combined. Divide mixture into 4 parts and gently form them into patties.

3. Broil or grill the patties about 5–6 minutes per side or until burgers reach desired doneness.

4. While the burgers are cooking, mix together the mayonnaise, garlic powder, paprika, and lemon juice. Set aside.

5. Serve each burger on a toasted bun with the garlic aioli, lettuce, onion, and tomato slices, along with coleslaw, baked beans, and a cold beer.

1 pound ground wild boar
⅓ cup crumbled feta cheese
2 tablespoons minced shallots
2 tablespoons fresh or bottled basil pesto
¼ teaspoon freshly ground black pepper

Garlic Aioli
⅓ cup mayonnaise
½ teaspoon garlic powder
½ teaspoon paprika
1 teaspoon lemon juice

4 whole-grain hamburger buns, split, buttered, and toasted
4 lettuce leaves
4 (¼-inch-thick) slices sweet onion (Walla Walla or Vidalia)
4 (¼-inch-thick) slices beefsteak tomatoes

Rack of Wild Boar with Fiery Apricot Sauce

You could also prepare this dish with peaches or nectarines, but I'd decrease the quantity to four or five since both fruits are larger than apricots. Wrapping the rack with bacon will make it more moist.

Serves 4

Fiery Apricot Sauce
2 red onions, minced
3 tablespoons olive oil
10–12 fresh apricots, skinned, pitted, and diced
1 teaspoon ground cumin
2 fresh jalapeños, peeled, chopped, and seeded
3 cloves garlic, minced
1 teaspoon lime zest
½ cup tequila
¼ cup apple cider vinegar
¼ cup lime juice
½ cup chopped cilantro
½ cup water
Pinch of salt

2 cups garlic croutons
2½–3 pound rack of wild boar (approximately 8 bones), silver skin removed, at room temperature
1 teaspoon kosher salt
½ teaspoon freshly ground black pepper
3 tablespoons olive oil
1 cup honey mustard

1. In a medium saucepan, sauté onions in olive oil. When soft, add apricots, cumin, jalapeños, garlic, lime zest, tequila, vinegar, lime juice, cilantro, water, and salt. Cook over medium heat until it boils, then simmer 20 minutes.

2. Let sauce cool, then run through a blender or food processor to purée; set aside. Grind garlic croutons in the processor until they become crumbs; set aside.

3. Preheat the barbecue or oven to medium-high (350–400°F) for direct heating.

4. With the boar at room temperature, season it generously on all sides with salt and pepper.

5. Place a large roasting pan or dutch oven on the hot barbecue, add olive oil to the pan, and heat until it's smoking. Add the boar, bone side up, and sear all surfaces until brown, about 12–15 minutes. Remove the boar.

6. Spread honey mustard evenly over the boar, including between each rib. Pat the crouton crumbs into the mustard to form an even crust.

7. Place the boar back into the pan and roast in the barbecue 10–12 minutes or until the meat is medium, with an internal temperature of 130°F.

8. To serve, place a heaping scoop of garlic mashed potatoes on each plate, top with 2 ribs, and drizzle everything with the apricot sauce.

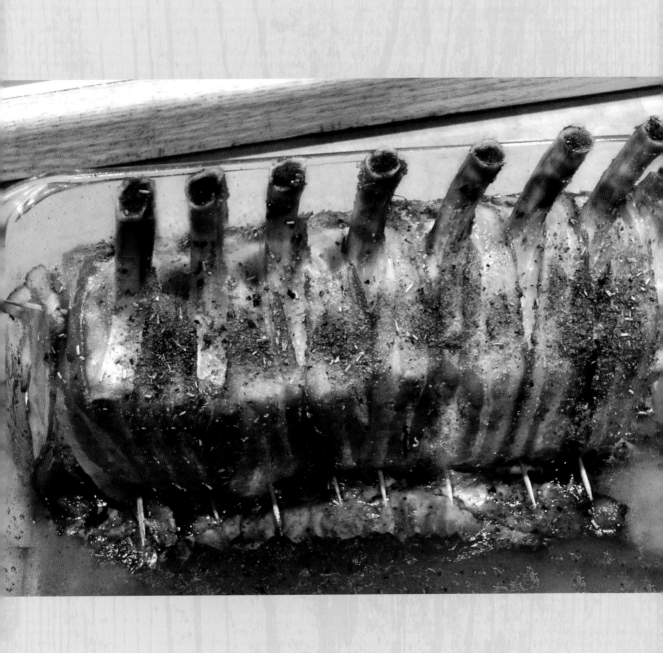

California Boar in Peanut Sauce

Never, ever, thaw frozen wild boar in a microwave—it will become tough and dry and be almost impossible to eat. Instead, thaw the meat by brining it in water, salt, and brown sugar, or let it thaw two or three days in the refrigerator.

Serves 6–8

3 tablespoons olive oil
2–3 pounds wild boar, cut into
   bite-size pieces
1 cup water
1 cup white wine
½ teaspoon kosher salt
Freshly ground black pepper
3 small tomatoes, peeled and
   chopped
3 Spanish onions, chopped
1 cup peanut butter (crunchy is
   best)

1. In a large dutch oven or roasting pan, heat olive oil until very hot, then add meat and sauté until browned on all sides. Reduce the heat and add water, wine, salt, and pepper; simmer 30 minutes.

2. Add tomatoes and onions and continue to simmer until the meat is done and is fork tender, about 15 minutes.

3. Spoon out some of the liquid and mix it with the peanut butter in a small bowl to make a smooth sauce, then add this to the meat mixture.

4. Continue to simmer on very low heat for another 20 minutes to fully integrate the sauce with the meat.

5. Serve with buttered noodles sprinkled with parsley and a rich rosé or blush wine.

Wild Boar Kabobs

If you want an extra-tender loin, brine this meat in 50 percent wine/50 percent water for eight to ten hours before cooking. The acidic wine helps break down the tissue and will produce a more tender and moist roast.

Serves 4–6

1 (14-ounce) can beef broth
2 tablespoons cornstarch
2 tablespoons soy sauce
1 tablespoon light brown sugar, packed
2 cloves garlic, finely minced
½ teaspoon ground ginger
1½ pounds wild boar loin, lean, cut into 1-inch cubes
Mushrooms
1 each medium red, yellow, and green bell peppers, cut into squares
1 large red onion, cut into wedges

1. Preheat the barbecue to medium-high (350–400°F), making sure the grill is well-oiled or sprayed.

2. In a saucepan, combine broth, cornstarch, soy sauce, brown sugar, garlic, and ginger. Bring to a boil, stirring constantly. Reduce the heat and continue to cook, stirring, until thickened.

3. Arrange wild boar cubes on skewers, alternating with mushrooms, peppers, and onion wedges. Grill 20–30 minutes or until done, frequently turning and brushing with the sauce.

4. Serve with baked beans and grilled corn on the cob.

Small Game

Stewed Swamp Gator

If you're using frozen alligator meat from an online website, make sure you thaw it in the refrigerator. The thawed meat should have no odor and be white, with no discoloration.

Serves 4

2 tablespoons butter

1 large green pepper, chopped

1 large onion, chopped

2 large shallots, minced

2 stalks celery, chopped

4 cloves garlic, diced

1 (16-ounce) can diced tomatoes

½ cup red wine

1 teaspoon Worcestershire sauce

1 teaspoon Louisiana Hot Sauce

1 tablespoon lemon juice

1 teaspoon balsamic vinegar

1 tablespoon oregano

½ teaspoon red pepper flakes

½ teaspoon Cajun seasoning

½ teaspoon kosher salt

½ cup flour

1½ pounds alligator meat, cut into bite-size pieces

1. In a dutch oven or roasting pan, melt butter over medium-high heat. Add peppers, onions, shallots, and celery and sauté until tender, about 10 minutes.

2. Add garlic, tomatoes, red wine, Worcestershire sauce, hot sauce, lemon juice, balsamic vinegar, oregano, red pepper flakes, Cajun seasoning, and salt and bring to a boil.

3. Put flour in a brown paper bag and add alligator meat a handful at a time, shaking to lightly flour the meat. Continue until all the meat is coated, then add the meat to the pot and stir.

4. Cover, lower heat to medium-low (250–300°F), and simmer, stirring occasionally, for 20–25 minutes or until the meat is very tender when pierced with a fork. If the meat begins to look dry and liquid is evaporating too fast, add ½ cup water or wine and continue cooking.

5. Serve over a bed of dirty rice accompanied by sautéed green beans.

Grilled Gator Kabobs

I've used alligator tail meat for this dish, but you can use any cuts as long as you chop them into cubes for the kabobs. I like to serve the kabobs whole on rice, with a few extra kept ready for second helpings.

Serves 4

1. Preheat the barbecue to medium-high (350–400°F), making sure grill is well oiled or sprayed.

2. In a 2-gallon resealable plastic bag, combine orange juice and concentrate, lime juice and zest, Worcestershire sauce, soy sauce, brown sugar, green onions, cumin, and red pepper flakes, and drop in alligator pieces. Marinate for at least 2 hours and up to 4 hours in the refrigerator.

3. Remove the alligator pieces from the marinade. Pour the marinade into a saucepan and boil for 10 minutes while the alligator comes to room temperature.

4. Thread marinated alligator cubes onto skewers, alternating with chunks of pineapple. If you can, use metal skewers, but if all you have are wooden ones, soak them in hot water for 20 minutes to help prevent them from burning.

5. Grill the kabobs for 6–8 minutes, turning once. Brush the kebobs with the boiled marinade while they are cooking, reserving the remaining marinade to serve at the table.

6. Serve the gator kabobs with spicy rice, grilled vegetables, and very cold beer.

¼ cup fresh orange juice
¾ cup orange juice concentrate
Juice of 1 lime
Zest of 1 lime
1 tablespoon Worcestershire sauce
3 tablespoons soy sauce
3 tablespoons brown sugar
2 green onions, green and white parts, chopped
1 teaspoon ground cumin
¼ teaspoon red pepper flakes
1½ pounds Florida alligator tail meat, cut into 2-inch cubes
1 small pineapple cut into 2-inch cubes

Teriyaki Frog Legs with Mushrooms

Frog legs are high in protein—an average serving has 16 grams—and low in fat, only 0.3 gram. They have the consistency of whitefish but taste like delicate chicken.

Serves 4

¼ cup butter

2 cups chopped onions

1 cup chopped red or green bell pepper

1 cup freshly minced parsley

1 pound sliced crimini mushrooms

2 tablespoons minced garlic

1½ teaspoons onion salt

½ teaspoon ground ginger

1 teaspoon favorite hot sauce

2 cups boned frog legs

½ cup dry white wine

½ cup teriyaki sauce

Minced green onions, green parts only, for garnish

1. In a large wok or skillet, melt butter over medium-high heat. Add onions, bell peppers, and parsley, sautéing until onions are clear.

2. Add mushrooms, garlic, onion salt, and ginger; stir well and cook until mushrooms are hot.

3. Add hot sauce and frog legs and stir well, then pour in the wine and teriyaki sauce.

4. Reduce the heat to medium-low (250–300°F) and simmer 10 minutes, stirring once or twice.

5. Garnish with minced green onions, and serve with buttered grits and stewed tomatoes.

Fried Frog Legs

When you purchase fresh or frozen frog legs, they should be firm and have no smell whatsoever. They are available on many websites and can usually be found at Asian grocery stores. Or you can catch them yourself at a local pond.
Serves 4

1½ pounds frog legs, rinsed
1 teaspoon salt
Freshly ground black pepper
2 eggs
1 cup milk
¼ cup flour
¼ cup cornmeal
1 teaspoon ground cumin
1 teaspoon curry (mild or hot)
¼ cup olive oil
1 lemon, cut in half
Paprika for garnish

1. Pat frog legs dry with paper towels. Season with salt and pepper.

2. In a medium bowl, beat eggs lightly with milk. Mix flour, cornmeal, cumin, and curry in a brown paper bag.

3. Dip the legs, 2 or 3 at a time, in the eggs, then place the legs in the bag and shake until they are covered in the seasoned flour-cornmeal. Set floured legs aside and continue until all legs are coated.

4. In a deep saucepan, heat olive oil until it just begins to smoke. Slip the legs into the hot oil and cook, turning once or twice, until they are very lightly browned and crispy, about 5 minutes for each batch.

5. Place the frog legs on a warmed serving tray, squeeze lemon halves over them, sprinkle with paprika, and serve hot.

Possum and Sweet Potatoes

As far as I know, you cannot buy possum anywhere on the Internet, so you'll either have to harvest one yourself or find someone who hunts them and will give you one. I had possum once and it tasted like strong dark chicken meat.

Serves 4

4 large sweet potatoes
1 possum, cleaned, skinned, and
    cut into pieces
½ pound bacon, roughly chopped
3 cloves garlic, minced
8 leaves fresh basil, chopped
1 tablespoon oregano
1 teaspoon seasoned salt
1 teaspoon freshly ground
    black pepper
2 cups beer
2 tablespoons brown sugar stirred
    into 1 cup melted butter
Fresh chopped parsley for garnish

1. Preheat the barbecue grill or oven to 350°F.

2. In a saucepan, boil sweet potatoes in their skins until they just become fork tender but not soft. Remove and let cool.

3. Place possum meat in a sprayed dutch oven or roasting pan, then add bacon, garlic, basil, oregano, salt, and pepper and stir to combine. Add beer, stir again, cover, and place in the barbecue or oven to bake 1½–2 hours or until meat is falling apart. Ladle pan juices over the meat 3 or 4 times. If the liquid gets very low, add more beer.

4. Peel the cooled sweet potatoes and drizzle the butter–brown sugar mixture over them; stir gently so as to not break them up. Add to the dutch oven, again stirring gently to mix the meat and potatoes, replace the cover, and cook another 50–60 minutes or until the meat falls from the bone.

5. Remove the cover and brown the meat for 15–20 minutes, and then ladle into wide bowls for serving, sprinkle with fresh parsley, and serve.

Valencia-Style Rabbit Paella

According to the custom in Valencia, you are supposed to add two or three dozen escargot (snails) in their shells to the paella at the same time you add the rice—we'll leave that up to your discretion. Personally, I think the snails add a delicious and authentic touch.

Serves 4

Olive oil, enough to cover the bottom of the paella pan
4 pound chicken, cut into breast, wing, thigh, and leg portions
3–4 pound rabbit, quartered
1 teaspoon kosher salt
¾ cup large white lima beans, uncooked
1 cup wide green beans, uncooked
2 medium ripe tomatoes, chopped
1 teaspoon sweet red paprika
8 cups hot chicken broth or stock
3 cups Spanish rice
1 teaspoon saffron

1. In a paella pan or wok, heat olive oil. When it is hot, add rabbit and chicken, sprinkle with salt, and fry until lightly browned.

2. Remove meat from the pan, drain well. Let the meat cool so you can handle it, then cut the meat off the bones into bite-sized pieces. Return the cooked meat to the pan, then add the white lima and green beans and cook them together wtih the meat.

3. While the meat and beans are cooking, clear an area in the center of the pan and fry the chopped tomatoes in it until they look a little pasty. Add paprika, stirring quickly, and immediately add hot chicken broth until it is almost to the top of the pan.

4. Cook all the ingredients about 20 minutes over high heat, then add the rice and saffron, stirring it throughout the pan, making sure that all of the rice is covered with liquid. Do not stir the rice after that. Keep the heat on high, keeping the liquid at a boil. It takes about 20 minutes for the rice to cook.

5. When all the broth is absorbed, take the paella pan or wok off the heat and let stand about 10 minutes, covering the top with a dish towel or newspaper. If the rice has been cooked correctly, the grains should be loose, not clumped together or mushy in texture.

6. The traditional way to eat paella is to put the pan in the middle of the table, give everyone a long wooden spoon, and serve with a loaf of French or Italian bread to tear into pieces and sop up the juices.

City Tavern Braised Rabbit

Chef Walter Staib is an award-winning, internationally known chef with over four decades of experience in restaurants in Europe, South America, Asia, and the Caribbean. Today he heads the internationally recognized City Tavern in Philadelphia, where he specializes in early American colonial cuisine. This recipe is from his recent cookbook, *The City Tavern Cookbook.*

Serves 8

5 pounds rabbit legs, skinned

3 cups full-bodied red wine (such as Burgundy), divided

1 sprig fresh rosemary

1 sprig fresh sage

6 whole peppercorns

½ cup vegetable oil

4 tablespoons unsalted butter, divided

4 stalks celery, chopped

2 carrots, peeled and chopped

1 large onion, chopped

3 cloves garlic, chopped

1 bay leaf

6 cups prepared brown sauce

3 tablespoons chopped fresh parsley

1 sprig fresh thyme, stemmed and chopped

2 medium zucchini, trimmed and chopped

½ small red cabbage, chopped (about 1 cup)

1 cup sliced white button mushrooms

2 large plum tomatoes, seeded and chopped

Salt and freshly ground black pepper

Egg noodles for serving

1. Cut each rabbit leg in half at the joint. Place the pieces in a medium bowl and add 2 cups wine, rosemary, sage, and peppercorns. Cover with plastic wrap and marinate in the refrigerator for at least 4 hours or overnight.

2. Remove the rabbit from the wine, discard the marinade, and pat the rabbit dry with paper towels.

3. Heat oil and 2 tablespoons butter in a large skillet over high heat, add the rabbit, and cook on all sides about 3 minutes, until brown. Reduce the heat to medium. Add celery, carrots, onions, and garlic and sauté until the vegetables are softened, about 5–8 minutes.

4. Stir in the remaining cup of wine, bay leaf, brown sauce, parsley, and thyme. Bring to a boil over high heat, then reduce the heat to medium-low (250–300°F) and simmer until the rabbit is tender but no longer pink, about 20 minutes. Remove from the heat and set aside.

5. Heat the remaining 2 tablespoons of butter in a large skillet over medium heat, then add zucchini and cabbage and sauté 5 minutes until al dente. Add mushrooms and tomatoes and cook until the mushrooms are just softened, about 5 minutes more.

6. Return the rabbit to medium heat, stir in the sautéed vegetables, and simmer about 5–7 minutes.

7. Season with salt and pepper and serve on a large platter of egg noodles.

Braised Rabbit Legs with Red Cabbage

According to the USDA, "Rabbit is an all-white meat that's lower in cholesterol than chicken or turkey (164 mg of cholesterol in rabbit vs. 220 mg in chicken), has just 795 calories per pound (chicken has 810 calories per pound), and has the highest percentage of protein and the lowest percentage of fat of any meat. In short, meat doesn't get any healthier."

Serves 4-6

4 7–8 ounce rabbit legs
2 apples, cored, peeled, and
    chopped
1 stalk celery, chopped
1 medium onion, coarsely chopped
2 tablespoons apple cider vinegar
1 tablespoon sugar
1 teaspoon kosher salt
8 cups water
1 tablespoon cracked black pepper

Red Cabbage
4 cups shredded red cabbage
1 cup sliced onions
¼ cup red wine vinegar
½ cup water
⅓ cup sugar
⅛ teaspoon ground cloves
1 teaspoon kosher salt
3 tablespoons butter
2 cups apples, cored, peeled,
    and thinly sliced

1. Place rabbit, apples, celery, onions, vinegar, sugar, salt, and water in a large dutch oven. Bring ingredients to a boil over high heat, then reduce to low and simmer 1 hour, uncovered.

2. Combine cabbage, onions, vinegar, water, sugar, cloves, salt, butter, and apples in a large pot, cover, and cook 20–25 minutes over low heat, stirring occasionally. Uncover and cook an additional 10–12 minutes or until most of the liquid has evaporated. Remove pot from the heat, cover again, and keep warm.

3. Remove rabbit from the dutch oven, season with cracked black pepper, and then place each leg on a bed of the cooked red cabbage on individual plates. Serve with buttered potatoes or noodles.

Fried Rabbit with Hard Cider Creamy Gravy

Wild rabbit can sometimes have that "gamey" taste people mention but often can't describe. If you're worried about it, marinate the rabbit in milk for six to eight hours before cooking, then discard the marinade.

Serves 4

2 tablespoons olive oil
1 tablespoon bacon fat or lard
¼ cup plus 2 tablespoons flour, divided
1 teaspoon ground cumin
1 teaspoon garlic powder
1 teaspoon oregano
1 fryer rabbit, cut into serving pieces
1 tablespoon salt
2 teaspoons freshly ground pepper
1½ cups warm water
1½ cups hard apple cider
1 clove garlic, minced
1 sprig fresh rosemary
3 tablespoons flour
¼ cup half-and-half

1. Heat olive oil and bacon fat in a heavy covered skillet or dutch oven over medium-high heat until a drop of water flicked in it sizzles. In a wide, flat pan, mix ¼ cup flour, cumin, garlic powder, and oregano.

2. Dredge each rabbit piece in the seasoned flour and put in the skillet to brown on both sides. Don't overcrowd the pan; instead, fry in 2 batches. Salt and pepper each batch as it cooks.

3. Place all of the rabbit back in the pan. Add water and hard apple cider, enough to cover the meat, then add garlic and rosemary. Simmer, covered, about 1 hour or until rabbit is tender.

4. In a small bowl, mix flour and half-and-half and set aside.

5. Remove the cooked rabbit pieces to a heated serving platter and cover, then increase the heat under the skillet to bring the liquid to a full boil. Reduce the heat and add the flour and half-and-half, stirring constantly until the mixture is thick and creamy.

6. Ladle the cream sauce over the rabbit pieces and serve with cheesy garlic mashed potatoes and steamed broccoli.

Southern Roasted Raccoon

It's very important, if you are dressing your own coon, that you remove the four scent glands, two of which are found deep in the pit under each foreleg and two below the tail. Care should be taken not to cut into glands or the meat will be spoiled and inedible. Raccoon meat properly cooked tastes like a very good pork roast.

Serves 4–6

1. Remove all visible fat from the carcass of the raccoon and cut into quarters.

2. Place the coon in a pot of water and add garlic salt; soak the meat for 24 hours.

3. Drain, rinse the meat in cold water, and put the meat in another pot with enough water to cover it by 2 inches. Bring the water to a rolling boil, then reduce the heat and simmer the meat 50–60 minutes, until it is just beginning to get tender.

4. Preheat the oven to 375°F.

5. Place stuffing mix in a bowl, add chicken or vegetable stock, and stir to mix and moisten the stuffing. Place stuffing on the bottom of a well-oiled or sprayed dutch oven or roasting pan.

6. Place the raccoon pieces on top of the stuffing, season with pepper and salt, and cover with salt pork or bacon. Bake, uncovered, 1 1/2–2 hours or until meat is very fork tender.

7. Serve the raccoon quarters alongside the stuffing, providing barbecue sauce on the side for the meat. I love this with fried okra or succotash with bacon.

5–6 pound young raccoon, dressed and trimmed
1 tablespoon garlic salt
1 (6-ounce) package chicken or turkey stuffing mix
1 cup chicken or vegetable stock
1 teaspoon pepper
1 teaspoon seasoned salt
1 pound salt pork, in thin slices, or bacon
Favorite smoky barbecue sauce

Rattlesnake in Lentils

To add a little "bite" (sorry, I couldn't resist), you can mince a jalapeño pepper and add it to the Crock-Pot with the snake meat.

Serves 4–6

1½–2 pounds rattlesnake meat

4½ cups water

2 tablespoons fresh lemon juice

1 large onion, chopped

2 tablespoons freshly minced garlic

2 tablespoons finely chopped fresh parsley

1 (14.5-ounce) can diced tomatoes

¼ cup finely diced carrots

2 bay leaves

1 teaspoon salt

1 teaspoon black pepper

½ teaspoon paprika

1 teaspoon thyme

1 teaspoon ground cumin

1 tablespoon rosemary

1 cup dry lentil beans

1. Simmer rattlesnake in water and lemon juice for 1 hour. Remove and separate the meat from the bones.

2. Combine the boned meat with the rest of the ingredients in a Crock-Pot and slow-cook 6–8 hours, or bring to a boil in a large stockpot and simmer 2 hours.

3. Serve with toasted garlic bread.

Snapping Turtle Stew

The common snapping turtle inhabits lakes and streams from South America to Canada, and in some parts of the United States, primarily in the South, it is commonly cooked and eaten. It sometimes has a strong flavor, more like beef than chicken.

Serves 6-8

2 tablespoons butter
1 tablespoon olive oil
2 pounds snapping turtle meat,
    cut into 1-inch pieces
2 quarts water
1 large onion, sliced
1 tablespoon minced garlic
2 cups chopped celery
1 cup chopped carrots
2 cups frozen lima beans, thawed
1 (16-ounce) can sliced potatoes
1 tablespoon thyme
½ teaspoon kosher salt
½ teaspoon freshly ground black
    pepper
2 tablespoons cornstarch
¼ cup good-quality sherry
3 tablespoons freshly minced
    parsley for garnish

1. Melt the butter with the oil in a dutch oven or roasting pan, and brown the turtle meat on all sides over medium-high heat, about 8–10 minutes.

2. Add 2 quarts of water and bring to a boil, then add the vegetables, thyme, salt, and pepper. Turn the heat down to low and simmer 45–55 minutes or until the meat is tender.

3. To thicken the stock, mix 2 tablespoons cornstarch with 2 tablespoons cold water and stir to blend. Then add a bit at a time to the hot liquid (not boiling) and stir until desired thickness is reached.

4. Just before serving, add the sherry to the stew, stir once or twice, and garnish with parsley. Serve in heated bowls with garlic bread and extra sherry to add to the soup.

Fowl

Cumin and Cola Doves

For a different marinade, try using orange or mandarin orange soda instead of the cola, and replace the honey with three tablespoons of orange marmalade.

Serves 4 as appetizers

8 doves
1 (16-ounce) bottle cola
1 tablespoon oregano
1 teaspoon ground cumin
½ teaspoon onion powder
1 tablespoon crushed fresh
   rosemary leaves
1 teaspoon lemon or citrus salt
½ teaspoon freshly ground
   black pepper
16 slices hickory-smoked bacon
1 tablespoon olive oil
4 lemon quarters

Barbecue Sauce
½ cup reserved cola marinade
½ cup soy sauce
2 tablespoons honey
¼ cup ketchup

1. Place doves in a 2-gallon resealable plastic bag and pour in the bottle of cola. Seal the bag, shake to mix, and refrigerate 2–3 hours.

2. Remove the doves from the cola and let them come to room temperature, about 20 minutes. Pour the cola marinade into a saucepan and boil 10 minutes. Set aside to cool.

3. In a small bowl, mix oregano, cumin, onion powder, rosemary, salt, and pepper; set aside.

4. Pat the birds dry, sprinkle them with the seasonings, and then wrap each bird with 2 bacon slices. Secure with toothpicks.

5. Mix all the ingredients for the barbecue sauce together in a small bowl; set aside.

6. In a cast-iron skillet, heat the olive oil and brown the birds over high heat, about 15 minutes. Pour half of the barbecue sauce over the birds, cover the pan, and cook another 15 minutes. Birds should be very tender.

7. Serve on small plates with lemon quarters to squeeze over the doves, along with a sauceboat of the remaining barbecue sauce to pour over the birds at the table.

Wild Duck with Pecan-Raisin-Currant Stuffing

Instead of the raisins and currants, you can substitute dates, apples, apricots, prunes, or pears, or a combination of several dried fruits.

Serves 4

4 (1.5–2-pound) wild ducks, dressed and cleaned
4 cups panko or fresh soft bread crumbs
1 cup minced onions
1 cup minced celery
½ cup golden seedless raisins
½ cup dried currants
1 cup pecan halves
2 eggs, beaten
¼ cup milk
12 slices bacon
½ cup ketchup
¼ cup balsamic vinegar
½ cup bottled chili sauce
3 tablespoons Worcestershire sauce
¼ cup chopped parsley for garnish
¼ cup Craisins (dried cranberries) for garnish

1. Rinse ducks thoroughly with water and pat dry. Preheat the barbecue or oven to 350°F.

2. In a medium bowl, combine bread crumbs, onions, celery, raisins, currants, pecans, eggs, and milk, and stir to mix well.

3. Spoon the mixture into the duck cavities, closing them with skewers or sewing them shut with butcher's twine.

4. Place ducks, breast side up, on a rack in a roasting pan. Wrap 3 slices of bacon around each duck and secure with toothpicks. Bake, uncovered, 1 hour.

5. Combine ketchup, vinegar, chili sauce, and Worcestershire sauce and stir to mix well. Pour over the ducks and bake for an additional 15–20 minutes or until desired degree of doneness. A thermometer inserted into the thick part of the breast should read 180°F.

6. Remove ducks to a serving platter and cover with foil. Skim off fat from the pan sauce and pour or spoon the sauce into a sauceboat to serve with the ducks.

7. Garnish the ducks with chopped fresh parsley and Craisins and serve.

Plum Sauce Duck

To make the green onion brushes used in this recipe, trim the roots from the onions and, using a sharp knife, cut them into 2-inch-long pieces. Then cut vertically into the onion stalk about 1 inch, making a deep cross, and repeat so that the onion is quartered into a four-segmented "brush."

Serves 4

Marinade
1 cup sparkling wine
1 cup honey
½ cup Chinese plum (hoisin) sauce
1 teaspoon garlic powder
1 tablespoon ground ginger
¼ teaspoon salt

1 5–6 pound wild or domestic duck
1 bunch green onions, white part
 and first 2 inches of green part
½ cup Chinese plum (hoisin) sauce,
 to serve with duck
Mandarin pancakes

1. Mix the marinade ingredients in a large bowl and set aside.

2. Wash and dry the duck, then place it in a 2-gallon resealable plastic bag, add the marinade, seal the bag, and refrigerate overnight.

3. The next morning, take the duck out of the bag and drain off the marinade. Reserve the marinade, putting it in a covered container and either freezing or refrigerating it. Using twine or butcher string, make a loop through both wings and hang the duck from a cabinet, ceiling fixture, or pot rack over a wide pan. Let dry for 1 day.

4. When it's time to cook the duck, put the reserved marinade in a saucepan and boil 10 minutes; cool and set aside to use to baste the duck. Preheat the barbecue to medium (400–500°F).

5. Place the duck on a rack in a roasting pan and generously prick the duck all over with a sharp fork. This will help the fat under the skin to melt and drip away, as the skin has pulled away from the meat due to the marinade drying and tightening the skin surface.

6. Place the duck in the barbecue and cook 2–2½ hours, until a meat thermometer in the breast registers 160°F. Baste occasionally with the boiled marinade and rich duck fat pan drippings.

7. When the duck reaches the desired temperature, take it off the barbecue, baste once more with a thick coat of marinade/basting sauce, wrap loosely in foil, and let rest 10 minutes.

8. To serve, you can carve the duck as you would a chicken, or, better yet, prepare and present it the Chinese way by cutting the duck skin and meat into bite-size pieces and serving with hoisin sauce, green onion brushes, and mandarin pancakes (available in packages at most Asian food stores). Use a green onion brush to spread hoisin sauce on the pancakes, add a piece of duck skin and a piece of duck meat, fold or wrap it up, and eat.

Beaux Tie Duck

The Vietnamese or Thai fish sauce used in this recipe is pungent and strident, but adds a wonderful flavor profile to the duck. If you can't find it or don't want to use it, substitute soy sauce.

Serves 4

1 4–5 pound duck
1 quart apple cider

Green Beans
1 large onion, sliced
½ pound green beans, ends trimmed
1 tablespoon freshly grated ginger
1 tablespoon minced garlic
½ teaspoon red pepper flakes
1 teaspoon kosher salt
½ teaspoon freshly ground black pepper
1 tablespoon brown sugar
2 tablespoons *nuoc mam* fish sauce
2 tablespoons lime juice, or to taste
Coarsely chopped fresh cilantro leaves

1. Remove the excess fat from the duck and place the duck in a resealable plastic bag. Pour in the apple cider and marinate overnight in the refrigerator.

2. Preheat the barbecue to 350–400°F for indirect heating, putting a water pan under the unheated side of the grill.

3. Remove the duck from the marinade and let it come to room temperature; discard the marinade.

4. In a large bowl, combine onions, green beans, ginger, garlic, and red pepper flakes and mix well. Sprinkle with salt and pepper, brown sugar, then add fish sauce and stir again; set aside.

5. Place the duck on a roasting rack over indirect heat on the grill, and cook until the internal temperature in the breast reaches 180°F, about 1–1½ hours.

6. Thirty minutes before you think the duck will be done, pour the green bean mixture into a roasting pan and place in the oven at 375°F. Cook until tender, stirring occasionally.

7. Remove the duck from the grill, cover with foil, and set aside to rest. Remove the green beans and place 2–3 generous scoops on each plate, sprinkle with the lime juice and cilantro leaves, and place ¼ of the duck on each plate. Accompany with stir-fried or steamed rice.

Beer Butt Duck on a Cedar Plank

This fun way to cook a duck guarantees a moist and tender bird. The Cold Duck (or other blush or white wine) steams the duck from the inside, while the heat and smoke from the barbecue cook it from the outside. The beer butt cedar planks can be ordered online. You can also make this dish without the plank by setting the duck and can in a shallow baking dish, adding ½ inch water to the pan.

Serves 2–3

1 (4–5 pound) duck

Marinade
¼ cup olive oil
2 tablespoons lemon juice
2 tablespoons orange juice
2 teaspoons dried thyme
1 teaspoon kosher salt

6–8 ounces inexpensive red wine

Sauce
1¼ cups dried cherries
2 tablespoons brandy
½ cup orange juice
1 cup dry red wine
⅓ cup balsamic vinegar
1½ cups chicken stock
Zest of 1 orange

1. Wash and dry duck, set aside. Combine olive oil, lemon juice, orange juice, thyme, and salt in a resealable plastic bag and add the duck. Marinate in the refrigerator overnight, turning occasionally.

2. Place an empty soft drink or beer can in the hole in a beer butt chicken cedar plank and soak in water overnight, weighing it down so it stays under the water.

3. Preheat the barbecue to 350°F, then distribute coals or briquettes on the bottom of the barbecue, leaving the middle uncovered. Place a water pan in the center and fill with 1 inch of water.

4. Drain the duck well and reserve the marinade. Remove the cedar plank from the water and pat dry, fill the empty can half-full with wine, and slide the duck tail-side down over the can.

5. Place the plank in the center of the grill and cook 1½–2 hours, until the internal temperature in the breast reaches 180°F on an instant-read thermometer. Boil the marinade for 10 minutes; you can then use it to baste the duck while it cooks.

6. While the duck is cooking, prepare the sauce by soaking the cherries in the brandy and orange juice in a small bowl for about 20–30 minutes. Then pour the cherries and juices into a medium saucepan, add the wine, and bring to a boil over medium-high heat. Lower the heat and simmer 3–4 minutes, uncovered. Add the vinegar and simmer 2–3 more minutes. Add the chicken stock and turn up the heat to medium-high to reduce the liquid by half, about 8–10 minutes. Remove the pan from the heat and keep warm.

7. Carefully remove the cedar plank and place it on a heatproof countertop. Carefully remove the duck from the very hot can and transfer it to a cutting board, cover with foil, and let rest 10 minutes. Save the plank to reuse.

8. Cut the duck in half or quarters and place on a heated plate. Ladle the cherry sauce over each piece, and sprinkle orange zest over all. Serve with shoestring fried potatoes and honey-glazed carrots.

Drunken Ducky

You could also use a fruity white wine like a Gewürztraminer or Riesling in this recipe, but save the expensive vintages to drink, not mix with soup and stuffing.

Serves 3–4

1 (10.5-ounce) can cream of mushroom soup
1 (10.5-ounce) can cream of chicken soup
6–8 duck breasts (3–4 ounces each), boneless and skinless
1 (6-ounce) package chicken stuffing mix
2 cups blush wine
1 tablespoon poultry seasoning
1 teaspoon minced garlic
Paprika for garnish

1. Preheat the oven to 350°F.

2. In a large bowl, stir the soups together to combine. Pour half of the mixture into a buttered or sprayed baking dish. Place the duck breasts on top of the soup mixture, then cover the duck with the rest of the soup.

3. In another bowl, combine the stuffing mix and wine, stirring to soak all the stuffing cubes. Sprinkle with the poultry seasoning and garlic and stir again.

4. Spoon all of the stuffing over the duck in the pan, covering it completely.

5. Bake 45–60 minutes or until the duck is done and a thermometer inserted into the thick part of the breast reads 160°F. If the stuffing begins to brown too quickly, cover with a sheet of aluminum foil.

6. Depending on the size of the duck breasts, place 1 or 2 on each plate on top of mashed sweet potatoes, and garnish with a sprinkle of paprika.

Duck Bites

You could also use a slice of cantaloupe, fresh apricot, or apple instead of the jalapeño pepper. If so, add a pinch of red pepper flakes to the dressing for a tiny kick.
Serves 6–8

1. Remove the skin from duck breasts and cut the meat into 1½- to 2-inch cubes. Place 1 shrimp and 1 1-inch piece of jalapeño on each cube and completely wrap in 1 slice of bacon.

2. Insert a toothpick through the bacon, shrimp, pepper, and duck meat; set aside until all pieces are prepared.

3. Place the bacon-wrapped duck cubes in a large bowl and add the dressing, gently folding to incorporate every piece. Cover the bowl with plastic wrap and refrigerate overnight.

4. Preheat the barbecue to medium-high (350–400°F), making sure the grill is completely oiled or sprayed.

5. Remove and briefly drain the bacon-wrapped duck cubes. Grill the cubes, turning several times until the bacon is cooked and browned all over.

6. Serve as an appetizer or luncheon entrée. Serve with a green salad, dirty or wild rice, and lots of cold beer.

4–6 duck breasts
¼ pound small shrimp, peeled and deveined
3 fresh jalapeños, cut into 1-inch pieces
1 pound hickory-smoked sliced bacon
1 (16-ounce) bottle Catalina or Russian dressing

Duck with Kirschwasser

Kirschwasser, or cherry brandy, is a colorless fruit brandy made by double-distilling a member of the sour cherry family. It's often referred to by its shortened name of Kirsch in the United States and Germany.

Serves 4

4 (6-ounce) duck breasts, boneless

Seasoning
½ teaspoon seasoned salt
Freshly ground black pepper
    to taste
1½ teaspoons chopped fresh
    thyme
½ teaspoon dried basil
½ teaspoon chopped fresh
    rosemary

1 tablespoon olive oil
½ cup finely chopped shallots
½ teaspoon granulated garlic
½ cup Kirschwasser (cherry brandy)
½ cup chicken stock
1 cup chopped dried cherries
1 tablespoon honey
2 tablespoons butter
2 tablespoons minced chives
    for garnish

1. Score the fatty side of the duck breasts and lightly season both sides with half of the mixed seasoning ingredients.

2. Heat olive oil in a large skillet over medium-high heat, then add the duck breasts and sear the skin side 4 minutes. Turn and cook the other side 2 minutes for medium-rare. Remove duck from the skillet and cover to keep warm. Reserve 1 tablespoon of the fat.

3. In a saucepan, sauté shallots and garlic in the reserved fat, cooking 1 minute while stirring constantly so the garlic doesn't burn. Add Kirschwasser, stock, cherries, honey, and remaining seasoning and bring to a simmer, scraping up any browned bits clinging to the bottom of the pan.

4. Cook until the cherries are plump and the liquid is reduced to a thick sauce, about 3–4 minutes. Add butter, stirring constantly to incorporate. Return the duck breasts to the pan with any pan juices and cook over low heat 1–2 minutes until the duck and sauce are warmed through.

5. Transfer the duck breasts to 4 serving plates and spoon the sauce and cherries over each portion. Garnish with the minced chives and serve with or over wild rice.

Partridge with Orange Slices

It used to be the fashion for hunters to hang game birds by the neck, and when the body fell off the head, it was deemed ready to cook. Perhaps a bit too gamey for us today, but hanging in a cool, airy place for a day or two actually will help the flavor of most game birds.

Serves 4

4 partridge breasts
2 tablespoons olive oil
Kosher salt and freshly ground
    black pepper
4 (¼-inch-thick) slices orange,
    seeded
8 slices bacon
Chopped parsley for garnish

Basting Sauce
¼ cup butter, melted
Grated peel of 1 orange
3 tablespoons fresh orange juice
1 tablespoon fresh lemon juice

1. Preheat the barbecue or oven to medium-high (350–400°F).

2. Rub partridge breasts with olive oil and sprinkle with salt and pepper. Place 1 slice of orange on each breast and wrap with 2 slices of bacon; either tie with butcher string or use toothpicks to anchor.

3. Place the breasts on a sprayed or buttered baking pan. Roast 15–20 minutes or until tender, basting frequently with combined butter, orange peel, orange juice, and lemon juice.

4. Remove string or toothpicks. Garnish the partridge with the roasted orange and bacon slices and a sprinkle of parsley.

Green Chili Grouse Stew

Grouse and partridge are interchangeable in these recipes, as they are very similar in size, taste, and preparation methods. The most commonly hunted grouse in the United States and Canada are the ruffed grouse, dusky grouse, spruce grouse, and sage grouse.

Serves 4–6

2 grouse, cut into breasts and thighs
1 large Spanish onion, roughly chopped
1 teaspoon freshly minced garlic
1 teaspoon dried oregano
1 teaspoon dried rosemary
½ teaspoon ground cumin
1 tablespoon cornstarch
1 tablespoon water
1 (14.5-ounce) can chopped tomatoes
1 4-ounce can chopped green chilies (mild or hot)
Minced parsley, paprika, or minced chives for garnish

1. Remove skin and bones from breasts and thighs and soak overnight in salt water (2 tablespoons salt to 1 gallon cold water).

2. Pour out the salt water and rinse the meat. Place the meat in a deep saucepan, cover with 3 cups water, and simmer until the meat easily breaks apart, about 30 minutes.

3. Remove the meat from the water, reserving the poaching liquid. Drain the grouse pieces well, cut into 1- to 1½-inch pieces, and set aside.

4. Add onions, garlic, oregano, rosemary, and cumin to the poaching stock and simmer 10–15 minutes. Make a paste out of the cornstarch and water and add it to the saucepan, stirring until thickened. Add tomatoes, green chilies, and the grouse pieces. Simmer for a few minutes, making sure the stew does not get too thick.

5. Ladle the stew into bowls and sprinkle with minced parsley, paprika, or diced chives. Serve with Indian fry bread or warmed and buttered tortillas.

Grouse Tagine

A tagine pot consists of two parts: a round pot (traditionally clay) and a conical cover with a small hole, which allows some steam to escape. Or you can use a dutch oven, leaving an opening when you cover the pot.
Serves 4–6

1. In a small bowl, combine the seasoning ingredients and stir to mix. Brush the grouse pieces with 2 tablespoons olive oil, rub half of the seasoning onto the grouse, then place the pieces in a resealable plastic bag, seal, and refrigerate overnight.

2. Preheat the barbecue or oven to 350–400°F.

3. Heat 6 tablespoons olive oil in a tagine or dutch oven over medium-high heat and sauté the grouse pieces until nicely browned. Add the remaining seasoning, garlic, and onions, and continue to heat 2–3 minutes while stirring.

4. Add chicken stock and bring to a boil; reduce heat, cover (if using a dutch oven, leave a small opening for steam to escape), and simmer 25–30 minutes.

5. Add raisins, olives, apricots, prunes, tomatoes, and preserved lemon slices and stir to blend. Simmer 20 minutes, stirring occasionally.

6. Remove grouse pieces with a slotted spoon and keep warm. Continue cooking sauce until it reaches a thickness you like—it should at least coat the back of a spoon.

7. Place grouse pieces on a heated platter and cover with the sauce. Serve with wild rice or couscous.

Seasoning
1 teaspoon black pepper
1 teaspoon ground ginger
1 teaspoon ground cumin
1 teaspoon turmeric
¼ teaspoon ground cinnamon
1 teaspoon coriander

2–3 (3-4-pound) grouse (or partridge), cut into serving-size pieces
8 tablespoons olive oil, divided
3 cloves garlic, minced
2 onions, finely chopped
2 cups chicken stock
½ cup raisins
½ cup olives
½ cup dried apricots
½ cup prunes
1 cup stewed tomatoes
2 whole preserved lemons, cut into thick slices

Grouse in Sour Cream

For a little extra kick, you can stir ¼ cup brandy or Grand Marnier into the gravy just before serving.

Serves 4–8

½ cup flour
1 teaspoon garlic salt
½ teaspoon lemon pepper
1 teaspoon sage
1 teaspoon rosemary
4 grouse, halved
2 cups sour cream, room
   temperature
½ cup chicken or vegetable broth
2 tablespoons cranberry jelly
8 tablespoons butter, divided
6 tablespoons olive oil, divided
4 large green onions, green and
   white parts, chopped
½ pound crimini mushrooms,
   roughly chopped

1. Preheat the barbecue or oven to medium (300–350°F) for indirect heating.

2. Put flour, salt, lemon pepper, sage, and rosemary in a brown paper bag and shake to mix. Add the bird halves one at a time, and shake to lightly coat them with seasoned flour. Combine sour cream, broth and jelly and stir to mix. Set aside.

3. In a dutch oven or large roasting pan over medium-high heat, sauté the grouse halves in 3 tablespoons butter and 3 tablespoons olive oil in two batches. Turn once or twice until both sides are lightly browned. You should only do 4 half birds at a time, unless you have a very large pan. When first batch is browned, remove the birds to a platter, then add the same amount of butter and oil and sauté the rest of the grouse.

4. Remove the grouse and sauté the green onions and mushrooms in the same pan, using the remaining 2 tablespoons butter, cooking until the mushrooms are soft.

5. Return the grouse to the pan and add sour cream mixture and stir. Cover and bake in the barbecue or oven over indirect heat for about 1 hour.

6. Serve with roasted or steamed potatoes, green peas or beans, and a green salad.

Brandied Mandarin Partridge

This dish would work just as well using chukar, game hens, quail, or grouse. The only suggested adjustment would be if you are substituting quail, double the number of birds and halve the cooking time. And, of course, you can substitute apricots, nectarines or peaches for the mandarin oranges.

Serves 4

4 gray partridge
¼ cup flour
8 tablespoons butter, divided
2 tablespoons olive oil
½ cup marmalade
½ teaspoon kosher salt
½ teaspoon ground cumin
1 (16-ounce) can mandarin
    oranges, drained
3 tablespoons brandy

1. With a sharp knife, cut each partridge into 4 serving pieces, using breasts and legs, reserving the small wings and back to use later for stock.

2. Put flour in a small brown paper bag and add the partridge pieces, shaking to lightly flour them.

3. Melt 4 tablespoons butter with olive oil in a large deep skillet or dutch oven and add the partridge pieces, browning them over medium-low (250–300˚F) heat. It should take 20–25 minutes to brown all pieces on all sides.

4. When nicely browned on all sides, remove the birds to a platter. Add marmalade, 4 tablespoons butter, salt, and cumin to the drippings in the skillet, and stir until the jelly melts and is fully incorporated.

5. Return the partridge to the skillet, spooning the sauce over each piece. Add half of the mandarin oranges, cover the skillet, and simmer until the meat is fork tender, about 10–15 more minutes.

6. Skim off the fat with a spoon, then add the brandy, stir 1 minute, and serve. I love to serve this garnished with the rest of the mandarin oranges, over a combination of white and wild rice or a thick polenta to which you've added some chopped chives.

Baked Pheasant with Oyster Dressing

For a different taste, use sausage instead of the oysters, replacing the oyster liquor (or liquid in the can) with chicken or vegetable stock.

Serves 4

2 young pheasant
¾ cup chopped celery
¾ cup chopped onions
½ cup chopped carrots
1 cup margarine or butter
3 cups chopped oysters
2 cups oyster liquor—liquid in
    bottled or canned oysters
10 cups dry bread crumbs
2 eggs, beaten
1 tablespoon poultry seasoning
1 teaspoon kosher salt
1 teaspoon freshly ground
    black pepper
2 tablespoons olive oil

1. In a large stock or soup pot, boil pheasant in water 40–50 minutes or until tender.

2. In a skillet over high heat, sauté celery, onions, and carrots in margarine or butter until soft; set aside.

3. Preheat the oven to 350°F. Drain oysters, reserving the liquor. If you don't have 2 cups, add some water from the pheasant cook pot to make that amount.

4. In a large bowl, thoroughly mix the oysters, oyster liquor, celery-onion-carrot mixture, bread crumbs, eggs, poultry seasoning, sprinkle with half of the salt, and pepper.

5. Cut off the wings of the birds and reserve them. Season the insides of both birds with the remaining salt and pepper and fill with the stuffing mix. Brush the birds with olive oil and place them in a buttered or sprayed roasting pan.

6. Place any remaining dressing on a sheet of aluminum foil and place the wings on top of the stuffing, fold the aluminum foil into a package, and place alongside the birds in the pan. Bake 45 minutes, until lightly browned and leg joint moves easily and when clear liquid runs out if pierced.

7. Remove the birds to a cutting board, cover with foil, and let rest 10 minutes. Serve ½ bird to each person. Serve with rice to which you've added chopped apricots, peaches, golden raisins and sautéed onions, alongside glazed carrots or braised endive.

Curried Pheasant

If you're cooking a pheasant you or a friend shot, please be extra careful to remove all remaining shot pellets. It's no fun to bite down on a piece of steel shot. Only your dentist will be happy.

Serves 4–6

2 teaspoons coriander
1 tablespoon ground cumin
2 tablespoons sesame seeds
1 tablespoon turmeric
¼ teaspoon freshly grated ginger
2 teaspoons salt
3 pheasant, disjointed
3 tablespoons butter
1 cup sliced onions
1 cup water
1 cup white wine

1. Using a mortar and pestle or a clean coffee grinder, combine coriander, cumin, sesame seeds, turmeric, ginger, and salt, and process to a powder.

2. Rub mixture into pheasant pieces and let dry-marinate 1 hour.

3. Melt butter in a roasting pan or dutch oven, add onions, and sauté until tender. Add the pheasant and brown on all sides.

4. Stir in water and wine; cover and poach over low heat 20 minutes or until tender.

5. Remove the pan from the heat and cover, letting the pheasant rest 10 minutes to allow the internal juices to recirculate.

6. Serve with pesto pasta and a chilled Chianti or Valpolicella.

Pheasant Burgers

Try these on your guests without telling them you're serving them pheasant. Let them guess after their first bite!

Serves 4–6

1. Place strips of pheasant breast in a grinder or food processor and process to burger consistency.

2. In a medium bowl, combine the ground pheasant, onions, egg, bacon, oregano, paprika, thyme, and bread crumbs and mix thoroughly. Shape into 4–6 patties with your hands.

3. In a large frying pan over medium heat, sauté the burgers 5–7 minutes on each side in olive oil or bacon grease; cook to an internal temperature of 140°F.

4. Butter and toast hamburger buns. Place a thin slice of sweet onion and a slice of tomato on each bun, add the patties, and serve with your favorite condiments.

Breasts from 2 pheasants, boned
½ medium onion, chopped
1 large egg, beaten
6 slices maple-favored bacon, finely chopped
1 teaspoon oregano
1 teaspoon paprika
1 teaspoon thyme
1 cup fresh bread crumbs or panko
1½ teaspoon olive oil or bacon grease
4–6 hamburger buns
4–6 slices sweet onion
4–6 slices tomatoes

Honey-Roasted Pheasant

If you wish to have a bit stronger flavor, you can hang the pheasant in a cool, dark place for two or three days before cooking.

Serves 4

1 cup honey
1 cup creamy peanut butter
¼ cup cider vinegar
¼ cup dark soy sauce
¼ cup minced green onion
1 teaspoon salt
2 pheasant, cut in half through backbone

1. Preheat the barbecue or oven to 350°F.

2. In a medium saucepan over medium-low heat (250–300°F), combine honey, peanut butter, vinegar, soy sauce, green onions, and salt. Cook, stirring frequently, until the peanut butter is melted and the sauce is smooth.

3. Place pheasant halves in a 2-gallon resealable plastic bag and pour in the sauce. Seal the bag, shake to distribute evenly, and refrigerate overnight.

4. Place the pheasant in a casserole dish or roasting pan that you've generously buttered or sprayed and bake 50–60 minutes, basting frequently with the drippings.

5. Remove and serve immediately, placing half a bird on each plate and drizzling with the sauce. This dish goes well with brussels sprouts and wild rice.

Pheasant Stroganoff

You can also prepare this dish with grouse, ptarmigan, partridge, wild turkey, goose, or even duck.

Serves 4

2 pheasant, cut in pieces
3 cups buttermilk
10 slices bacon
1 cup flour
1 tablespoon honey mustard
1 teaspoon savory
½ teaspoon citrus pepper
1 teaspoon kosher salt
1½ cups chicken stock
3 tablespoons butter
4 large onions, chopped
¼ pound mushrooms, sliced
1 cup sour cream
2 tablespoons minced parsley
¼ cup sherry

1. Place pheasant pieces in a 2-gallon resealable plastic bag and pour in the buttermilk. Seal the bag and refrigerate overnight.

2. Remove the pheasant from the buttermilk and allow to drain and come to room temperature, about 20 minutes.

3. Fry bacon in a nonstick pan until crisp. Remove and drain the bacon, reserving the grease, then crumble and set aside.

4. In a medium bowl, combine flour, mustard, savory, pepper, and salt and stir to mix. Put the flour mixture in a brown paper bag, then add the pheasant pieces, 2 or 3 at a time, and shake to lightly flour the bird.

5. In a cast-iron skillet or dutch oven, heat 2 tablespoons of the bacon grease. Place the pheasant pieces in the skillet in 2 or 3 batches, adding grease between batches, and brown well on both sides. Remove the pheasant to a paper towel–covered platter to drain.

6. Wipe the skillet, add the pheasant pieces, and pour in the stock. Bring to a boil, cover, and reduce to a simmer. Simmer the pheasant until the meat is tender.

7. In another skillet, melt the butter and sauté the onions and mushrooms until tender. Remove the onions and mushrooms when tender and set aside.

8. When the pheasant is tender and lightly browned on all sides, add the onion-mushroom mixture, sour cream, and parsley to the skillet. Stir once or twice to combine, then cook on very low heat for 5 minutes; do not boil or sour cream will curdle. When you remove from the heat stir in the sherry.

9. Place the pheasant on top of buttered noodles, drizzle with half of the sauce, reserving the rest for serving at the table.

Marrakesh Grilled Quail

If doing a light lunch, one quail per person is adequate, but for dinner you should serve at least two quail per person, three for a big eater.

Serves 4

1 teaspoon cinnamon
1 teaspoon ground cumin
1 teaspoon ground coriander
1 teaspoon freshly ground black
　　pepper
¼ teaspoon ground cloves
1 tablespoon paprika
½ teaspoon red pepper flakes
1 tablespoon ground ginger
1 teaspoon kosher salt
2 cups chopped fresh cilantro
1 tablespoon freshly minced garlic
¼ cup extra-virgin olive oil
8 semi-boneless quail

1. In a small bowl, combine all the ingredients except the quail, and mix thoroughly.

2. Rub the spice paste all over the quail, then put them in a resealable plastic bag and marinate in the refrigerator 6–8 hours.

3. Prepare the barbecue for indirect heat at 350°F, placing a water pan under the grill.

4. Lightly oil the grill grate, season the quail with additional salt (to your preference), and grill about 5–6 minutes, turning once halfway through the cooking time. Don't overcook or the quail will become very dry.

5. I like to serve with couscous and steamed broccoli or brussels sprouts.

Savory Quail Kabobs

Serve these quail kabobs over wild rice or risotto, with grilled asparagus and tomatoes.

Serves 4

Marinade

1 cup molasses

1 cup orange juice

2 tablespoons minced garlic

2 tablespoons freshly grated
     ginger

1 teaspoon seasoned salt

1 teaspoon freshly ground black
     pepper

8 quail, boned

8 crimini mushrooms

4 (¾-inch-thick) pineapple slices

8 cloves elephant garlic

4 slices smoked bacon, cut in half

1. In a 2-gallon resealable plastic bag, combine all the marinade ingredients. Add the quail and mushrooms, seal the bag, and shake to combine. Refrigerate overnight.

2. Remove the quail and mushrooms from the marinade, reserving the liquid. Let the birds come to room temperature, about 1 hour. While the birds are resting, boil the reserved marinade for 10 minutes, then cool to use as a baste for the kabobs.

3. Preheat the barbecue to medium-high (350–400°F). Make sure the grill is clean and generously sprayed with nonstick grilling spray.

4. Skewer the quail, pineapple slices, marinated mushrooms, and garlic cloves (each wrapped in ½ slice of bacon), dividing the ingredients evenly between 4 metal kabob skewers. Brush the food with marinade while the kabobs grill, approximately 5 minutes per side.

5. Serve with pan-fried potatoes, grilled corn on the cob, and a green or fruit salad.

Fried Quail with Spicy Peach Chutney

If you would like a spicier meal, add two or three habanero peppers to the chutney and half a teaspoon of cayenne to the flour.

Serves 4

Chutney
8 medium ripe peaches, peeled and diced
Juice of 2 limes
2 fresh jalapeños, seeded and diced
1½ tablespoons freshly grated ginger
4 cloves garlic, minced
½ cup brown sugar
¼ cup unsweetened coconut flakes
½ teaspoon kosher salt

4 quail, dressed, partially boned if possible
1 quart cold water mixed with 6 tablespoons salt
1 cup whole-milk buttermilk
1 cup self-rising flour mixed with 1 teaspoon oregano
½ quart peanut or vegetable oil

1. In a medium saucepan over medium heat, add the chutney ingredients, stir, cover, and simmer 20 minutes. Remove the cover and simmer an additional 10 minutes to evaporate more of the liquid. Cool and place in a covered container in refrigerator until ready to use.

2. Place quail in a re-sealable plastic bag and cover with the salted water. Seal bag and refrigerate 6–8 hours.

3. Remove the quail from the bag and drain, discarding the salt water. Let the birds come to room temperature, about 25–30 minutes.

4. Pour buttermilk into a shallow dish, and spoon seasoned flour into another. Dip birds first in milk, then in flour; repeat. Set the floured birds on a rack or plate and let dry 15 minutes.

5. In a deep cast-iron frying pan or dutch oven, heat peanut oil to 365°F (check temperature with a thermometer). Fry birds 2 at a time for 12–15 minutes—trying to cook too many in one batch will lower the oil temperature.

6. As the birds finish cooking, place them on a plate with paper towels and keep in a warm oven.

7. Serve 2 birds per person with 1 or 2 generous tablespoons of the peach chutney.

Quail Pie

This is a modern version of an original English recipe that I read about on a trip to England last summer. Not four and twenty blackbirds—the quail here are much more appetizing.

Serves 4

1. In a small bowl, combine pork, eggs, cheese, sugar, allspice, saffron, and salt.

2. Line a 9-inch pie dish with half of the pastry, and fill the pie shell with the pork mixture.

3. Preheat the oven or barbecue to 375°F.

4. Dredge quail in flour, lightly coating all the halves, then brown in butter, turning often until all sides are browned. In small bowl combine the egg yolk and milk to make an egg wash, set aside.

5. Remove the quail from the skillet and lay the halves on top of the pie filling. Pour the stock over the birds.

6. Cover the birds and filling with the second pie pastry, cut several slits in it to let steam escape, and brush with the egg wash.

7. Bake 35–40 minutes. Remove from the oven and let rest 5 minutes before serving.

1 pound (2 cups) ground pork
3 hard-boiled eggs, chopped
½ cup shredded cheddar cheese
1 tablespoon sugar
1 teaspoon allspice
⅛ teaspoon saffron
1 teaspoon salt
1 package refrigerated piecrust
    (2 crusts)
3 quail, cut in half
Flour for dredging
2 tablespoons butter
½ cup chicken or vegetable stock

Egg wash
1 egg yolk beaten
1 tablespoon milk

Bacon Barbecued Quail

If you wish to serve these as a main course, allow three for each gent and two for each lady, of course increasing the ingredients accordingly. They are a bit of work to eat, but worth the effort. If you buy the quail online, you can order partially boned birds (only leg bones left).

Serves 5 as appetizers

5 whole quail
1 (16-ounce) bottle favorite
   Italian salad dressing
1 tablespoon paprika
1 teaspoon ground sage
½ teaspoon garlic powder
Salt and pepper to taste
1 pound sliced bacon
1 tablespoon bacon grease or
   cooking oil
½ cup barbecue sauce

1. Place quail in a resealable plastic bag and marinate in dressing overnight.

2. Pat the quail dry, season with paprika, ground sage, garlic powder, and salt and pepper to taste, then wrap each bird with 2 or 3 bacon slices, matching up the ends on the same side of the bird.

3. Melt bacon grease or heat cooking oil in a large cast-iron skillet.

4. Add the birds to the skillet with the bacon seam side down. Cover and cook 15 minutes over medium-high heat. Turn, brush with barbecue sauce, and cook another 5-7 minutes. Test the birds with a fork; if they are not tender, cook an additional 2-3 minutes.

5. I serve these at the table on a bed of pico de gallo accompanied by flour tortillas, so people can remove the meat from the birds with a fork, mix with the pico de gallo, and wrap in a warm tortilla.

Snow Goose with Brandy Sauce

There is no better way on earth to cook potatoes than in goose fat, and with the added bacon drippings, the taste of common potatoes is elevated to culinary artistry.

Serves 6

Brandy Sauce
¾ cup honey
½ cup brown sugar
½ cup pinot noir or cabernet
1 teaspoon steak sauce
⅛ teaspoon cinnamon
¾ cup brandy

1 6–8 pound snow goose
1–2 teaspoons kosher salt
1 large onion, quartered
2 large apples, cored and
    quartered
2 large oranges, quartered
8–10 strips bacon
8 Yukon Gold potatoes, peeled
    and quartered

1. Preheat the barbecue or oven to 300°F.

2. In a small saucepan over medium heat, combine all the brandy sauce ingredients and heat while stirring. Cook 2–3 minutes, until the brown sugar has dissolved. Set aside and keep warm. (Makes 1¾ cups.)

3. Clean the goose thoroughly and pat dry inside and out. Sprinkle salt generously inside the cavity. Fill cavity with the onion, apple, and orange quarters.

4. Place the goose on a roasting rack in a dutch oven or large roasting pan. Prick the skin all over with a sharp fork, then completely cover the goose with bacon strips, securing them to the bird with toothpicks.

5. Bake the goose approximately 3 hours (about 30 minutes per pound) or until a meat thermometer inserted in the breast reads 140–150°F. After 1 hour, place the potatoes in the roasting pan, turning them with a spoon to coat all surfaces in the goose fat. Turn occasionally as the goose continues to cook.

6. During the last hour of cooking, baste with the brandy sauce. Remove the bacon when you have 30 minutes left, and baste occasionally at least twice more.

7. Remove the goose from the pan, cover it, and let it sit 10 minutes to recirculate the internal juices. If you wish, chop the bacon and sprinkle it over the golden brown roasted potatoes in the pan. Remove potatoes to serving platter and set aside, keeping the platter warm.

8. Place the roast goose on a cutting board and slice off the breast meat, separate the legs and thighs, and place all on a top of the potatoes on the heated platter. Drizzle some of the remaining brandy sauce on the goose, and serve the rest of the sauce at the table.

Wild Goose, Straw Mushroom, and Oyster Stew

Wild goose meat is very dark red and almost indistinguishable from roast beef after you slice it. Unlike its domestic kin, wild goose has almost no fat.

Serves 4–6

1. In a dutch oven or deep cast-iron skillet, heat olive oil over medium-low heat (250–300°F), then add flour and stir continuously until you have a dark brown roux. Do not stop stirring or it will burn.

2. Add onions, bell pepper, and celery, cooking until all the vegetables are soft and wilted. Add oregano, basil, water, and goose pieces, and cook over low heat 2 hours or until the meat becomes fork tender.

3. Add oysters (including liquor), shallots, mushrooms, and parsley, and simmer slowly until the edges of the oysters begin to curl, about 5-8 minutes.

4. Serve over white or wild rice or buttered and toasted French bread rounds.

½ cup olive oil
½ cup all-purpose flour
3 yellow onions, diced
1 red, green, or yellow bell pepper, diced
½ cup diced celery
½ teaspoon oregano
½ teaspoon chopped fresh basil
3 quarts hot water
1 4–6 pound goose, cut into 1–1½ inch pieces
1 pint oysters, including liquor
⅔ cup minced shallots
1 cup straw mushrooms
⅓ cup freshly minced parsley

Marinated Canada Goose Breast

Note this recipe's title: It's *Canada* goose, not *Canadian* goose. They live not only in Canada, but also in much of the northern United States, and are the largest members of the world's goose families, ranging up to 17 pounds.

Serves 3–4

1 cup red wine
1 cup Worcestershire sauce
½ cup soy sauce
¾ cup brandy, divided
2 tablespoons olive oil
1 teaspoon garlic powder
1 tablespoon brown sugar
1 teaspoon freshly ground
    black pepper
¼ teaspoon ground cumin
1 whole Canada goose breast,
    skinned

1. In a large bowl, mix wine, Worcestershire sauce, soy sauce, ½ cup brandy, and olive oil. Add garlic powder, brown sugar, pepper, and cumin and whisk together.

2. Place the goose breast in a 2-gallon resealable plastic bag and pour in the marinade, covering the breast. Seal the bag, shake to mix, and refrigerate overnight.

3. Preheat the barbecue or oven to medium-high (350–400°F).

4. Remove the goose from the marinade. Pour the marinade in a saucepan and boil 10 minutes while the meat comes to room temperature. Cover the marinade and keep warm.

5. Tightly wrap the goose breast in aluminum foil, sealing the edges together.

6. Cook 20–25 minutes, then open and check the breast—it should be medium-rare. Do not overcook, as this will make the meat dry.

7. Add ¼ cup brandy to the marinade, stir, and pour in a sauceboat.

8. Slice the breast into thin, ¼-inch sections, like London broil, and serve immediately with the brandy sauce.

Pan-Fried Goose Focaccia Sandwiches

You could also serve these on sesame hamburger buns, kaiser rolls, onion rolls, Texas toast, rye bread, or pumpernickel. The secret is to first toast the bread and then slather with garlic butter.

Serves 4

2–4 goose breasts
2 eggs
2 tablespoons milk
¼ cup all-purpose flour
1 teaspoon blackened seasoning
½ teaspoon sugar
½ teaspoon ground cumin
½ teaspoon kosher salt
1 tablespoon butter
1 tablespoon olive oil
4 focaccia bread rolls, cut in half
¼ cup softened butter mixed
    with 1 teaspoon garlic powder
    and ½ teaspoon minced fresh
    parsley

1. Slice raw goose breasts across the grain into thin, ¼-inch slices; set aside.

2. Whisk eggs and milk in a wide bowl. In another wide, flat bowl, combine flour, blackened seasoning, sugar, cumin, and salt and mix well.

3. Dip the goose strips in the egg mixture, then press into the flour mixture to coat both sides of all pieces.

4. Pan-fry the floured slices in butter and olive oil just until flour turns golden brown, 3–4 at a time so as not to crowd the pan. Remove with tongs to a warmed platter and finish cooking the remaining strips.

5. Toast focaccia rolls under the broiler or in a toaster oven, then generously spread with the butter-garlic-parsley mixture, and top with 2 or 3 slices of the fried goose.

6. Serve with cranberry and/or currant jelly, mayonnaise, and sliced onions and tomatoes on the side.

Note: Use commercially available blackened seasoning or make your own using the recipe on page 164.

Wild Goose Potpie

On a cold winter day, nothing tastes as good as a steaming potpie. Just for fun, you might try to keep the ingredients a secret—most people will think it's a beef pie—until after your family or guests have told you how much they loved this dish.
Serves 4–6

1. Preheat the oven to 375°F. Remove crusts from the refrigerator, open packages, and let come to room temperature, about 25 minutes.

2. Slice cooked goose breast into 1-inch slices, then cut into 1-inch square cubes. Set aside.

3. In a saucepan over medium heat, melt butter with olive oil, then add wine and carrots and cook 5 minutes. Add potatoes and cook another 5 minutes. Add celery, onion, and peas and cook 3 more minutes.

4. In a large bowl, combine the goose cubes and cream of mushroom soup and stir together. Add garlic, rosemary, and oregano and stir until well mixed. Add the cooked vegetables and stir once more so that everything is combined.

5. Slide one of the piecrusts into a 9-inch pie tin. Add the filling, spreading it evenly across the crust. Whisk together the egg yolk and cream in a small bowl, set aside.

6. Place the second crust on the pie and fold edges together, sealing edges with a fork dipped in cold water. Cut 3 or 4 vents in the pie with a sharp knife, and brush the top and edges of the crust with the egg wash.

7. Bake the pie 35–40 minutes or until crust is golden brown and pie is bubbling. If it looks like it's browning too quickly, cover with aluminum foil.

8. Remove the pie from the oven and let it rest 10 minutes before serving with a crisp green or fresh fruit salad.

1 package refrigerated 2-crust pie dough
1 1½–2 pound cooked goose breast
2 tablespoons butter
2 tablespoons olive oil
½ cup white wine
1 cup thinly sliced carrots
1 medium Yukon Gold potato, cut into ¼-inch cubes
½ cup minced celery
½ cup minced onion
½ cup peas (I prefer fresh, but frozen will do just fine.)
1 (15.5-ounce) can condensed cream of mushroom soup
½ teaspoon granulated garlic
1 teaspoon rosemary
1 teaspoon oregano

Egg wash
1 egg yolk
1 tablespoon cream

Roast Wild Turkey with Maple Butter Gravy

Wild turkey has a rich taste unlike its domestic cousins. It often tastes better when aged for a couple of days, and brining certainly helps, as its a lean bird. Use 1 cup salt and 1 cup brown sugar in 2 gallons of water. Soak the whole prepared bird in this overnight. Then drain and cook as below.

Serves 4–6

2 cups apple cider

$1/3$ cup and $1/4$ cup real maple syrup, divided

2 tablespoons chopped fresh thyme, divided

2 tablespoons chopped fresh marjoram, divided

$1/2$ teaspoon lemon zest

$3/4$ cup softened butter, divided

$1/2$ teaspoon kosher salt

Freshly ground black pepper

12–14 pound wild turkey, neck and giblets reserved

2 cups chopped onion

$1 1/2$ cups chopped celery

$1 1/2$ cups chopped carrots

3 cups chicken broth, divided

$1/3$ cup flour

1. Boil apple cider and $1/3$ cup maple syrup in a large heavy saucepan over medium-high heat until reduced to $1/2$ cup, about 20 minutes. Remove from heat. Mix in 1 tablespoon thyme, 1 tablespoon marjoram, and lemon zest. Add $1/4$ cup butter and whisk until melted, then season with salt and a few generous grinds of pepper. Cover and refrigerate until cold, about 2 hours.

2. Make maple butter by combining $1/2$ cup softened butter with $1/4$ cup maple syrup, stirring to fully incorporate. Chill until needed.

3. Preheat the oven to 375°F and position the rack in the bottom third of the oven.

4. Pat turkey dry with paper towels. Slide your hand under the skin of the turkey breast to loosen skin. Rub $1/2$ cup of the cider-syrup-butter mixture over the breast under the skin.

5. Rub the turkey with the remaining $1/4$ cup cider-syrup-butter mixture and place on roasting rack as below. (To stuff the turkey, spoon stuffing into the main cavity and rub $1/2$ cup of the cider-syrup-butter mixture over the outside of turkey, cover and refrigerate the remaining mixture to use later in the gravy.)

6. Tie the legs together loosely to hold the shape of the turkey and place the turkey on a roasting rack. Combine onion, celery, carrots, and reserved turkey neck and giblets on the bottom of a large roasting pan or dutch oven, sprinkling the vegetables with the remaining 1 tablespoon of thyme and marjoram. Pour 2 cups broth into the pan, then place the roasting rack in the pan.

7. Roast the turkey 30 minutes, then reduce the temperature to

350°F and cover the turkey with a brown paper grocery bag, which you've brushed with olive oil. Continue roasting until a meat thermometer inserted into the thickest part of the thigh registers 180°F or until juices run clear when the thickest part of the thigh is pierced with skewer, about 2½ hours for an unstuffed turkey, 3 hours for a stuffed turkey. While the turkey is roasting, baste occasionally with the juices in the bottom of the pan.

8. When cooked, transfer the turkey to a platter and cover with aluminum foil, letting it rest 20 minutes to recirculate the juices. Reserve mixture in the pan for gravy.

9. Pour vegetables and pan liquid through a strainer into wide bowl, and skim off the fat with a spoon. Add enough chicken broth to measure 3 cups of liquid, then pour into a large saucepan and bring to a boil.

10. In a small bowl, mix the maple butter with flour to form a smooth paste and then whisk the paste into the gravy. Boil, stirring often, until the gravy thickens and coats the back of a spoon. Season the gravy to taste, and present at the table in a sauceboat.

Cajun Wild Turkey Breast

This dish, *Dindon Gras,* or "fatted turkey," is popular during Mardi Gras in Louisiana and is usually served over rice. Wild turkey is extremely lean, so you may wish to wrap it in additional bacon strips, cook for 20–25 minutes, then discard this bacon. Chop the turkey into chunks then proceed with step 3.

Serves 4–6

1 pound bacon, diced into ¼-inch
  pieces
1 tablespoon Cajun poultry
  seasoning, divided
4 tablespoons butter, divided
1½ cups chopped onion
2-pound boneless turkey breast,
  cut into 1-inch chunks
4 tablespoons olive oil, divided
1 tablespoon Worcestershire
  sauce

1. In a large heavy skillet, fry the bacon till crisp and sprinkle it with half the Cajun seasoning. Drain, discard the grease, and set the seasoned bacon aside.

2. Wipe out the skillet with paper towels. Add 1 tablespoon butter and heat over medium heat until bubbling, then sauté chopped onions until tender. Remove onions with a slotted spoon and set aside.

3. In a large bowl, combine turkey, 2 tablespoons olive oil, Worcestershire sauce, and the rest of the Cajun seasoning.

4. In the same skillet, heat 3 tablespoons butter and the last 2 tablespoons of olive oil until sizzling. Add the turkey mixture, bacon, and onions and sauté until the mixture is nicely browned and tender.

5. Serve over rice with grilled vegetables and thick slices of garlic bread.

Gobbler and Goober Pizza

Since turkeys are sometimes known as gobblers, and in the South peanuts are sometimes called goober peas, I couldn't resist this as a recipe title.

Serves 2–4

½ cup cooked wild turkey meat

2 tablespoons olive oil, divided

1 medium flatbread or refrigerated pizza crust

¼ cup peanut sauce (satay)

½ cup sliced mushrooms

¼ cup chopped onions

3 tablespoons minced chives

½ cup shredded Monterey Jack cheese

½ cup grated Parmesan cheese

1. Preheat the oven or barbecue grill to 350°F.

2. In a small bowl, mix the turkey with 1 tablespoon olive oil.

3. Spread 1 tablespoon olive oil on the flatbread or pizza crust, and put in the oven or barbecue for 5 minutes. Remove and let cool while you turn the heat up to 400°F.

4. Top the flatbread or pizza crust with peanut sauce and cover with the turkey, mushrooms, onions, chives, and cheeses. Bake 10–15 minutes, until the cheese is melted.

Wild Turkey Enchiladas

This recipe is a great way to use leftover turkey or other wildfowl for a tasty luncheon or dinner entree. You could use corn tortillas, but we prefer the lighter flour tortillas.
Serves 4

2 tablespoons butter
1 medium onion, sliced
½ teaspoon garlic salt
Freshly ground black pepper
2 boiled or broiled wild turkey breasts, shredded
1 (4-ounce) can mild green chilies
3 (14-ounce) cans green chili sauce, divided
6 cups shredded cheddar cheese, divided
6–8 (10-inch) soft flour tortillas
1 cup chopped plum tomatoes
½ cup chopped green onions

1. Preheat the oven to 350°F.

2. In a medium saucepan, melt the butter and sauté the onions until tender, then stir in garlic salt and 2–3 generous grinds of pepper. Add the shredded turkey and stir.

3. Add green chilies and 2 cans green chili sauce, then add 1 cup shredded cheese and stir until melted.

4. Spray a wide, flat roasting pan or wide Pyrex dish with grilling spray. Place ¼ cup of the turkey mixture onto one tortilla, carefully roll it up, and place it in the cooking dish seam side down. Repeat this process until the mixture is gone.

5. Cover the enchiladas with the third can of chili sauce and entirely cover the top with the remaining cheddar cheese. Bake 30 minutes or until cheese topping is bubbling.

6. Remove from the oven and scatter the chopped fresh tomatoes and green onions on top. Serve with bowls of sour cream and guacamole, Mexican rice, additional flour tortillas, and a green salad.

Wild Rice and Turkey Soup

You could class this dish up a bit by using wild rice instead of the white rice and heavy cream instead of the half-and-half. But no matter what, make sure you use a good sherry, not a "cooking" sherry.

Serves 8

1. Heat oil in large deep saucepan or dutch oven over medium-high heat, and sauté carrots, onions, celery, and garlic 5 minutes or until vegetables are tender.

2. Stir in turkey, mushrooms, rice, stock, garlic salt, and pepper and cook 10 minutes, stirring occasionally. Add half-and-half and cook until heated through, stirring occasionally.

3. Ladle soup into serving bowls. Float 1 tablespoon sherry in each bowl, sprinkle with chopped parsley and serve.

1 tablespoon vegetable oil
2 large carrots, finely chopped
1 large onion, finely chopped
½ cup finely chopped celery
2 cloves garlic, minced
2 cups chopped leftover cooked turkey
1 cup sliced button mushrooms
2 cups cooked jasmine rice
2 (14.5-ounce) cans chicken stock
¼ teaspoon garlic salt
¼ teaspoon freshly ground black pepper
2 cups half-and-half
½ cup dry sherry
Chopped fresh parsley for garnish

Fish

Garlic Roasted Bass

This is a very simple dish, simply seasoned and grilled, that goes well with dirty or Mexican rice and grilled vegetables.

Serves 4

2 (1–1½-pound) whole striped bass (head and tail intact), cleaned
4 tablespoons olive oil, divided
8 cloves garlic, divided
1 lime, thinly sliced
2½ lemons
1 teaspoon kosher salt
1 teaspoon freshly ground black pepper

1. Preheat the barbecue to medium-high (350–400°F) for direct heating, putting a cast-iron or roasting pan on the grill to heat up. Or, if using an oven, heat to 400°F and preheat a large shallow baking or roasting pan in the oven.

2. Put the fish on a plastic cutting board and cut 4 deep slits (down to the bone) at an angle on each side of the fish. Brush the fish inside and out with 2 tablespoons olive oil. Cut 1 garlic clove in half lengthwise and rub all over the skin of the fish.

3. Thinly sliver the remaining garlic cloves and insert the slivers into the slits on both sides of the fish; you should have some left over to sprinkle inside the body cavity as well. Place the lime slices inside the fish, reserving a few for garnish.

4. Squeeze 1 lemon over both sides of each fish and generously season with salt and pepper. Reserve half of 1 lemon and cut into thin slices for garnish; set aside.

5. Spray the pan with grilling spray and place the fish in the middle of the pan; they should sizzle immediately. Drizzle the remaining 2 tablespoons olive oil over both fish and roast about 16–18 minutes, until the flesh flakes easily.

6. Serve the fish whole at the table, using a spatula and sharp knife to fillet them on the serving tray. To serve, remove the top fillet from each fish by cutting through the skin along the top edge of the backbone and along the belly, then remove the backbone to reveal the other fillets. Garnish with lemon and lime slices.

Bass with Buttered Leeks

Leeks are related to both onions and garlic but have a sweeter taste than most onions. They must be cleaned thoroughly because other than a four-year-old boy playing in the dirt, nothing attracts or hides as much dirt as leeks do.

Serves 4

1. Slice the white parts of the leeks into paper-thin slices. Wash well, then pat the leeks dry with paper towels.

2. In a large saucepan or roasting pan over medium-high heat, melt 2 tablespoons butter. Add the leeks, water, 3 tablespoons wine, and $1/2$ teaspoon salt. Bring to a quick boil, then reduce the heat to a simmer, cover, and cook 20–25 minutes.

3. Add $1/4$ cup wine to the saucepan, cover again, and cook 10 minutes longer. The leeks should be very soft and melted into a soft mass. Remove the pan from the heat and set it aside on a very low burner to keep warm.

4. In a very large nonstick skillet over medium-high heat, melt the remaining 3 tablespoons butter. Add the fillets to the skillet and cook until golden, turning once, about 3–4 minutes per side, making sure the fish is opaque throughout.

5. Place the fillets on a platter and pour the leek and butter sauce over the hot fish Sprinkle with the remaining kosher salt and a few grinds of black pepper, garnish with sprigs of fresh parsley, and serve.

4 large leeks (about $1 1/4$ pounds),
   white parts only
5 tablespoons butter, divided
3 tablespoons water
3 tablespoons plus $1/4$ cup white
   wine, divided
1 teaspoon kosher salt, divided
4 thick Chilean sea bass fillets
   (about 7 ounces each)
Freshly ground black pepper
Fresh parsley sprigs for garnish

Thai-Style Grilled Bass

I sometimes marinate the fillets in coconut milk for an hour before cooking, adding even more coconut flavor to the sauce.

Serves 8–10

Sauce

Zest and juice of 3 limes

3 tablespoons freshly grated ginger ¼ cup finely chopped leeks 1 tablespoon light soy sauce

½ cup coconut milk

3 tablespoons vegetable oil

4 cloves garlic, minced

2 tablespoons chopped green onions, green and white parts

Pinch of onion salt

3 pounds striped bass fillets

1. Preheat the barbecue to medium-high (350–400°F), making sure the grill is well oiled or sprayed.

2. In a medium bowl, whisk together the sauce ingredients until well combined.

3. Generously brush the fillets with the sauce and grill about 5 minutes each side or until the fish is opaque and flakes easily with a fork. Turn the fillets once and brush on the sauce several times while the fish cooks.

4. Ladle the sauce over the fish and serve with saffron-tomato rice and slices of orange, lime, or lemon as garnish.

Poached Bass

Mixing the stock and wine gives a richer-tasting poaching liquid than just wine or stock by itself. You can also add sliced onions or shallots to the pan to add yet another flavor dimension.

Serves 4

4 ounces chicken stock
4 ounces dry white wine
1 bay leaf
1 teaspoon Old Bay seasoning
½ teaspoon tarragon
1 teaspoon coriander
½ teaspoon lemon pepper
1 teaspoon paprika
Zest and juice of 1 lemon
½ teaspoon kosher salt
¼ teaspoon red pepper flakes
1¼ pounds thick sea bass fillets
Minced green onions for garnish,
    green and white parts

1. In a poaching pan or skillet with a lid, combine stock, wine, bay leaf, Old Bay, tarragon, coriander, lemon pepper, paprika, lemon zest and juice, salt, and red pepper flakes. Over medium-high heat, bring the liquid to 180°F. Do not boil.

2. Add the fish fillets and partly cover the pan, leaving some space for the poaching liquid to partially evaporate. Turn the fish once during cooking and spoon the liquid over the top of the fillets while they poach. Cook until an instant-read thermometer inserted into the thickest fillet registers 140°F, about 8–10 minutes.

3. Transfer the fillets to a platter and garnish with the minced green onions. Serve with grilled yellow and zucchini squash and steamed rice.

Mushroom-Shrimp-Stuffed Bass

Instead of shrimp, you can use crab, diced lobster, or scallops in this recipe, and if you have a favorite mushroom (straw, button, morel, and so on), you can use those instead of the crimini.

Serves 4–6

½ cup chopped shallots
¼ cup chopped celery
½ teaspoon tarragon
½ cup chopped crimini mushrooms
3 tablespoons butter
½ cup chopped cooked (51/60)
    cocktail shrimp
2 cups soft bread crumbs
1 teaspoon kosher salt
⅛ teaspoon freshly ground
    black pepper
2 pounds striped bass fillets
Juice of 2 lemons
3 large tomatoes, cut into
    ¼-inch slices
Freshly minced parsley for garnish

1. Preheat the oven to 375°F.

2. In a large saucepan, sauté shallots, celery, tarragon, and mushrooms in butter for 5–8 minutes, until the mushrooms are wilted and soft. Add shrimp, bread crumbs, salt, and pepper and stir to combine. Cook 1 minute, then remove from the heat and set aside.

3. Spray or butter a large shallow baking dish and arrange the bass fillets in the dish. Sprinkle with lemon juice, spread the stuffing over the fillets, and cover with tomato slices. Bake, uncovered, 35–40 minutes.

4. Remove the fillets from the oven, transfer to plates, sprinkle with freshly minced parsley, and serve.

Roasted Butterfish (Black Cod) with Cider and Leeks

In California black cod is known most often as butterfish. In the Pacific Northwest it's called smoked sable or smoked black cod, and in Alaska it's known simply as sablefish. Elsewhere, it's just black cod. Whatever it's called, it's loaded with omega-3 oil, hard to find in stores, hard to catch, but is utterly delicious.

Serves 4

1. Preheat the barbecue or oven to 375°F.

2. In a cast-iron skillet or roasting pan over medium-high heat, melt butter, add leeks and onions, and sauté 2–3 minutes until softened but not browned.

3. Add garlic and cider, then place the fillets on top of the leeks and onions, drizzle with olive oil, and season with salt and a few generous grinds of black pepper.

4. Roast in the barbecue or oven 10–12 minutes until the fish is cooked. The fillets should be opaque, only slightly browned on the edges, and flake easily with a fork.

5. Serve the fish on top of 2–3 tablespoons of the leeks and onions, sprinkle with paprika, and accompany with steamed and buttered potatoes and sautéed green beans.

¼ cup butter
3 leeks, trimmed and thinly sliced
1 medium onion, thinly sliced
1 teaspoon freshly minced garlic
1 cup pear cider
4 (6–7-ounce) butterfish (black cod) fillets, skinned and boned
2 teaspoons olive oil
½ teaspoon lemon salt
Freshly ground black pepper
Paprika for garnish

Honey-Grilled Sablefish (Black Cod)

This fish, aka Butterfish, has large pin bones, which are curved little bones that run along the fish's centerline. They need to be removed with needle-nose pliers before cooking.

Serves 4

4 (4–6 ounce) sablefish fillets, skinned and boned
2 tablespoons dark soy sauce
1 teaspoon honey
1 tablespoon freshly grated ginger
2 tablespoons soy sauce
Juice of 1 lemon
1 tablespoon butter
1 teaspoon minced shallots
1 cup fresh spinach, washed and patted dry
¼ teaspoon kosher salt
1 teaspoon minced lemon zest

1. Brush cod with soy sauce and marinate 5–10 minutes.

2. Preheat the broiler to 350°F.

3. Cover a roasting or broiler pan with aluminum foil and spray it well with grilling or cooking spray. Brush the fillets with honey and place on the pan. Broil 5–6 inches from the heat for 3–5 minutes, until the honey caramelizes and the fish is opaque throughout. Remove the fillets from the oven, cover with foil, and keep warm.

4. In a dry sauté pan over medium heat, cook ginger until it just begins to brown. Add soy sauce, lemon juice, and butter and heat until butter melts. Add shallots and cook 2 minutes, then stir in spinach, add salt, and cook until spinach wilts.

5. Transfer the spinach to a large heated platter and place the cod fillets on top. Garnish with lemon zest and serve.

Pinebark Stew (Catfish Stew)

This spicy fish stew, which is popular in the South (especially in the Carolinas and Georgia), has several theories surrounding its name. Some refer to the stew being either cooked over or served on pine bark, others relate to the color of the stew (dark brown), and yet another proposes that the early settlers learned the recipe from local American Indians.

Serves 8–10

1. In a stew pot or dutch oven, combine bacon, potatoes, tomatoes, onions, and water, and bring to a boil, then reduce the heat and simmer 1$\frac{1}{2}$ hours.

2. Add catfish, tomato sauce, thyme, salt, pepper, and ketchup (if using) and simmer an additional 20–30 minutes.

3. Serve in shallow soup bowls or over steamed rice.

8 ounces bacon, diced and cooked
 until crisp, then crumbled
5 large potatoes, peeled and diced
3 (15-ounce) cans stewed tomatoes
3 medium onions, minced
2 quarts water
3 pounds skinned catfish fillets,
 cut into 1-inch pieces
1 (8-ounce) can tomato sauce
$\frac{1}{2}$ teaspoon thyme
$\frac{1}{2}$ teaspoon salt
$\frac{1}{2}$ teaspoon ground black pepper
$\frac{1}{4}$ cup ketchup (optional)

Buttermilk Fried Catfish

Grouper, black sea bass, and tilapia can be substituted for catfish in most recipes.
Serves 4

8 catfish fillets (preferably
    4 ounces each)
1½ cups buttermilk
2 tablespoons garlic salt
½ teaspoon oregano
1 tablespoon freshly ground
    black pepper
1½ cups yellow cornmeal
½ cup flour
Bottle of favorite hot sauce

1. Rinse catfish fillets with cold water and pat dry.

2. Pour buttermilk in a wide, flat dish. Place the fillets in the buttermilk, cover the dish, and let the fish soak 2–3 hours in the refrigerator.

3. Put salt, oregano, black pepper, cornmeal, and flour in a brown paper bag.

4. Remove the fish from the buttermilk, and press each fillet into the seasoned flour on both sides.

5. Fry the fillets, 2 or 3 at a time, in a deep fryer or in a pan in at least an inch of oil heated to 325°F. In the deep fryer, the fish will float to the surface when done; in the pan, you must turn them after each side is browned, about 3 minutes per side.

6. Remove the fillets with a slotted spoon or spatula to a plate you've covered with several layers of paper towels to drain the grease. Serve with bottle of favorite hot sauce, hush puppies, green beans, and stewed tomatoes for a real Southern experience.

Blackened Catfish Fillets

Do not make this recipe in your kitchen. Believe me, you will regret it, and you will spend the next two days wiping soot off the walls, ceiling, light fixtures, cabinets, and almost every other vertical or horizontal surface of your kitchen! I know this from experience. Cook this dish *outside* on your barbecue grill.

Serves 4

6–8 catfish fillets

Blackened Seasoning
2 teaspoons cayenne pepper
1 teaspoon thyme
1 teaspoon oregano
1 teaspoon ground cumin
1 teaspoon paprika
1 teaspoon lemon pepper
1 teaspoon black pepper
1 teaspoon kosher salt
1 teaspoon garlic powder
1 teaspoon onion powder
¼ cup melted butter
1 cup Italian salad dressing

1. Preheat the oven to 350°F.

2. Rinse catfish fillets in cold water, then pat dry with paper towels.

3. Combine the seasoning ingredients in a small bowl, stirring well to thoroughly blend.

4. Pour melted butter into a wide, flat dish or bowl. Dip the catfish fillets in the butter, then heavily sprinkle both sides of the fillets with the seasoning. Reserve the remaining butter.

5. Heat a cast-iron skillet over high heat on an outside barbecue side burner until it is very hot. Pour the leftover butter into the skillet, place the catfish fillets in the skillet, and cook 2 minutes on each side until the fillets are slightly blackened and just beginning to char.

6. Remove the fillets from the skillet and lay them in the bottom of a sprayed or buttered baking dish. Brush the Italian dressing on each fillet and put in the oven for 20–25 minutes, until the fish easily flakes with a fork.

7. Serve the fillets over a bed of white steamed or dirty rice.

Catfish Po'boys

If you don't wish to make the coleslaw yourself, most grocery stores carry prepackaged shredded cabbage and carrots for coleslaw, and the folks at Kraft make a delicious coleslaw dressing that is also widely available. Use those instead of the first five ingredients.

Serves 4

Coleslaw
2 tablespoons mayonnaise
1 tablespoon sour cream
1 tablespoon white wine vinegar
1 teaspoon sugar
2 cups shredded cabbage and
    carrots (or prepackaged
    coleslaw mix)

¼ cup cornmeal
2 teaspoons Cajun seasoning
½ teaspoon onion salt
⅛ teaspoon cayenne pepper
¼ cup buttermilk
1 pound catfish fillets, cut into
    small pieces
2 teaspoons olive oil
4 hoagie rolls, split

1. In a small bowl, combine mayonnaise, sour cream, vinegar, and sugar and whisk until smooth. Add coleslaw vegetables and stir to combine. Set aside.

2. In a brown paper bag, combine cornmeal, Cajun seasoning, onion salt, and cayenne.

3. Pour buttermilk into a shallow bowl. Dip the fish in the milk, 2 or 3 pieces at a time, then drop them into the bag, close the bag, and shake to coat. Repeat until all the pieces are coated.

4. In a large nonstick skillet over medium heat, cook the catfish in olive oil for 4–5 minutes on each side or until the fish flakes easily with a fork and the coating is golden brown. Briefly drain on paper towels, keep warm in very low oven (200°F) until all fillets are cooked.

5. Put the catfish in the rolls and spoon on the coleslaw. Serve with french fries or hush puppies.

Grilled Flounder with Apple Salsa

You can order Mis' Rubins White Magic (or its cousin, Black Magic) online at www. misrubins.com or purchase it at your local upscale grocery market. Both White and Black Magic are wonderful and much more loaded with flavor than ordinary barbecue rubs or seasonings.

Serves 4

Salsa

4 Granny Smith apples, finely
    diced, unpeeled
2 teaspoons finely chopped
    orange zest
1 teaspoon finely chopped lemon
    zest
1 teaspoon finely chopped lime
    zest
¼ cup pineapple rum (or other
    flavor)
1 teaspoon finely minced fresh
    jalapeño
¼ cup chopped fresh cilantro
6 green onions, green and white
    parts, thinly sliced
1 cup cranberry jelly
½ teaspoon kosher salt
⅛ teaspoon freshly ground black
    pepper

4 (6–8 ounce) flounder fillets
¼ cup clarified butter with
    1 tablespoon lemon juice added
1 tablespoon White Magic
    seasoning
¼ teaspoon red pepper flakes
¼ teaspoon cayenne pepper
Lemon quarters and cilantro
    sprigs for garnish

1. Preheat the barbecue to medium-high (350–400°F).

2. In a large bowl, combine the salsa ingredients and mix well. Set aside.

3. Brush both sides of the flounder fillets lightly with clarified butter, then generously sprinkle the White Magic and red pepper flakes on both sides of the fillets, add a sprinkle of cayenne, and let rest 5 minutes.

4. Position a large sheet of oiled or sprayed aluminum foil on the grill. Slide the fillets onto the foil and cook about 2 minutes, then turn over to cook another 1–2 minutes. The fish will cook very quickly—be careful not to overcook it. When done, the flesh should just start to flake and be moist.

5. Garnish the flounder with lemon wedges and sprigs of cilantro, and serve accompanied by the apple salsa.

Cedar-Plank Halibut

Depending on the width of your halibut fillet, use one or two regular cedar planks, soaked and placed side by side, or cut fillet into plank-size pieces and cook on more than one plank.

Serves 4–6

1 teaspoon freshly grated
    lime zest
1 teaspoon freshly grated
    lemon zest
1 teaspoon kosher salt
1 teaspoon freshly ground
    black pepper
1 teaspoon minced chives
1 teaspoon ground thyme
2 2–3 pound whole butterflied
    halibut fillets
2 tablespoons olive oil
1 teaspoon paprika for garnish

Guacamole
½ cup mayonnaise
½ cup sour cream
1 large ripe avocado, skinned
    and pitted
1 garlic clove, minced
1 teaspoon chipotle powder
Juice of 2 fresh limes

1. Soak cedar plank 2–3 hours in hot water. Drain briefly, pat the top of the plank dry, brush it with olive oil, and set aside.

2. Preheat the barbecue to medium-high (350–400°F) for indirect heating, arranging the coals around the perimeter of the grill and putting a water pan in the center of the coals.

3. In small bowl, combine the lime and lemon zests, salt, pepper, chives, and thyme and stir to mix well. Drizzle halibut with olive oil and sprinkle with the mixed seasonings.

4. Place the halibut on the prepared cedar plank, place the plank in the center of the grill, and cook until the fish lightly flakes but is still somewhat translucent in the center, about 16–20 minutes. Keep a spray bottle of water handy to douse any flare-ups of the cedar plank.

5. Meanwhile, combine the guacamole ingredients in a food processor and pulse until smooth. Scoop into a small bowl, cover, and keep at room temperature.

6. Using oven mitts or barbecue gloves, remove the plank from grill, cover the fish lightly with foil, and allow it to rest 5 minutes.

7. Cut the fillets into serving-size pieces, place on lettuce leaves on a large platter, and sprinkle with paprika. Serve with warm flour (or corn) tortillas, guacamole, and lime wedges.

Halibut Cheeks on Squid Ink Pasta

If you've never had halibut cheeks, you're in for a culinary treat. Many people, including this author, think that simply and properly prepared, they taste like a cross between lobster and crab—no kidding. Give them a try!

Serves 4

1 pound halibut cheeks
¼ cup all-purpose flour
½ teaspoon garlic salt
½ teaspoon freshly ground
    black pepper
2 teaspoons butter
4 tablespoons olive oil, divided
1 pound squid ink pasta
⅓ cup white wine
1 teaspoon freshly grated
    lemon zest
3 tablespoons fresh lemon juice
1 clove garlic, minced
¼ cup freshly grated Parmesan
    cheese
¼ cup fresh parsley

1. Put a large pot of water (3–4 quarts with 1 tablespoon salt added) on the stove and bring to a boil.

2. Cut large cheeks into quarters if necessary. In a brown paper bag, mix flour, garlic salt, and pepper. Add the halibut cheeks, 3 or 4 at a time, and shake to flour each piece; continue until all the fish has been floured.

3. Heat butter and 2 tablespoons olive oil in a large skillet over medium-high heat. Add the halibut cheeks and cook 2 minutes on each side or until lightly browned. With a slotted spoon or spatula, remove the cooked cheeks from the pan, place on a heated platter, cover, and keep warm.

4. Add pasta to the boiling water and cook until al dente, about 3–4 minutes. Drain pasta, then put in a large bowl, sprinkle with the remaining olive oil, and toss to coat. Cover and keep warm.

5. In the same skillet you cooked the cheeks in, add white wine, lemon zest and juice, and garlic and cook 3 minutes over medium heat, stirring occasionally.

6. Remove the skillet from the heat and pour the contents over the pasta, tossing gently to coat. Gently fold in the halibut cheeks until well distributed through the pasta.

7. Transfer the pasta to wide, flat pasta bowls and sprinkle with Parmesan cheese and parsley. Serve with sliced garlic bread.

Grilled Halibut with
Crab and Shrimp Sauce

This recipe also works well with chunks of lobster or small bay scallops in place of the shrimp and crab.

Serves 4

¼ cup minced carrots

¼ cup minced celery

3 tablespoons extra-virgin olive oil, divided

2 tablespoons minced shallots ¼ cup white wine

6 ounces fresh crabmeat

6 ounces uncooked cocktail shrimp

3 tablespoons minced fresh parsley

2 tablespoons savory

1 teaspoon granulated garlic

Zest of 1 lemon, minced

2 tablespoons fresh lemon juice

1 ripe tomato, diced

1 tablespoon tomato paste

1½ pounds halibut fillet, skin on, about 1¼ inch thick

½ teaspoon kosher salt

5–6 fresh parsley sprigs for garnish

1. Preheat the barbecue to medium-high (350–400°F), making sure the grill is well oiled or sprayed.

2. In a saucepan over medium-high heat, sauté carrots and celery in 1 tablespoon olive oil until soft, about 5 minutes. Add shallots and heat another 3 minutes until they become translucent, stirring occasionally. Add wine and cook another 1–2 minutes to slightly reduce the liquid in the pan.

3. Remove the pan from the heat and add crabmeat, shrimp, parsley, savory, garlic, lemon zest and juice, diced tomatoes, and tomato paste. Stir to mix well and cook 2–3 minutes until shrimp are warmed through. Set aside and keep warm.

4. Cut the halibut fillet in half, cutting right through the heavy backbone and leaving it in place. Rinse and pat dry, then brush with the remaining olive oil and lightly sprinkle with salt. Grill the fillet 5 minutes on one side and 4 on the other.

5. To serve, carefully remove the halibut skin and bones and discard. Spread half of the crab-shrimp sauce on a warm platter and place the fillets on top, then top with dollops of the remaining sauce and some fresh parsley sprigs.

Blue Cheese Baked Halibut

For those who don't like blue cheese (too bad), you can substitute Swiss, cheddar, Monterey Jack, Pepper Jack, or another favorite cheese for the stronger blue.

Serves 6

1. Preheat the oven or barbecue to 350°F.

2. In a large bowl, combine all but 3 tablespoons of the blue cheese with the buttermilk, mayonnaise, wine, pepper, garlic, and paprika; add water to thin if needed. (It should lightly coat the back of a spoon dipped in it.) When thoroughly mixed, cover with plastic wrap and chill until needed.

3. Spray or butter a 9 x 13 x 2-inch pan. Pour half the blue cheese sauce into the pan and place the halibut on top of the sauce. Cover the fish with the remaining sauce, and top with red onion slices, the remaining 3 tablespoons of blue cheese, and dill.

4. Bake in the barbecue or oven until fish flakes easily, about 10–12 minutes.

5. Serve on individual plates or on a serving platter with cottage fries and grilled asparagus.

1 cup blue cheese crumbles, divided
½ quart buttermilk
1¾ cups mayonnaise
1 cup white wine
½ teaspoon freshly ground black pepper
1½ teaspoons minced garlic
½ teaspoon paprika
3 pounds halibut, cut into 5-ounce pieces
1 large red onion, sliced
2 tablespoons finely chopped fresh dill

Basil-Ginger Swordfish Steaks

As some varieties of swordfish are threatened, please only fish for or buy broadbill, Espanda, Emperador, and Shutome varieties of swordfish from Hawaiian and North American waters.

Serves 4

Marinade

¼ cup olive oil

Juice of 3 limes

1 tablespoon freshly minced garlic

¼ cup lightly packed fresh
    basil leaves

¼ cup freshly grated ginger

¼ cup coconut milk

4 (8-ounce, ¾-inch-thick) swordfish
    steaks

Herb Vinaigrette

3 tablespoons balsamic vinegar

¼ cup rice wine vinegar

1 teaspoon Dijon mustard

16 large fresh basil leaves

1 teaspoon savory

½ cup vegetable oil

½ teaspoon garlic salt

½ teaspoon citrus pepper

Grilled Vegetables

1 large Vidalia onion, cut into
    ¼-inch slices

6 green onions, green and white
    parts, cut into 4-inch pieces

1 large red bell pepper,
    cut into ¼-inch slices

1 large yellow bell pepper,
    cut into ¼-inch slices

1 cup sliced portobello
    mushrooms

3 tablespoons olive oil

½ teaspoon kosher salt

½ teaspoon freshly ground
    black pepper

1. Combine all the marinade ingredients in a food processor and pulse to combine. Put the steaks in a resealable plastic bag and pour in the marinade. Shake the bag to mix and refrigerate overnight.

2. To make the herb vinaigrette, combine the balsamic vinegar, rice wine vinegar, and mustard in a food processor and pulse briefly, then add the basil and savory and pulse again until coarsely chopped. With the processor running, add the vegetable oil very slowly to smoothly blend. Add salt and pepper; cover and set aside.

3. Preheat the barbecue to medium-high (350–400°F), making sure the grill is well oiled or sprayed.

4. Remove the swordfish steaks from the marinade. Pour the marinade into a saucepan and boil 10 minutes while the fish comes to room temperature.

5. In a wide bowl, toss the onions, bell peppers, and mushrooms with the olive oil, salt, and pepper.

6. Grill the swordfish until it is very lightly browned, with light grill marks on both sides and the interior is medium, about 3–4 minutes per side. While the fish is grilling, spread the vegetables along the perimeter of the grill and carefully cook until they are soft, with singed edges.

7. Remove the fish from the grill to warmed plates, drizzle the herb vinaigrette over the fish, and serve with the vegetables on the side.

Grilled Fresh Marlin with Mango-Pineapple Relish

If you wish, you can marinate the marlin steaks in some lemon juice, garlic, and olive oil for twenty to thirty minutes before cooking to make them a little bit more tender.
Serves 6

Mango-Pineapple Relish
1 tablespoon vegetable oil
¼ cup minced onion
1 small fresh jalapeño, seeded and minced
1 mango, peeled, pitted, and diced
½ cup chopped fresh pineapple
¼ cup roasted red peppers, diced
¼ cup tequila
Juice of 1 lime, freshly squeezed
1 tablespoon chopped fresh cilantro

6 (6-ounce) marlin steaks
2 tablespoons olive oil
½ teaspoon kosher salt
Freshly ground black pepper

1. In a small saucepan, heat oil over medium-high heat and sauté onions until translucent and wilted, about 3–4 minutes. Add jalapeño, mango, and pineapple and sauté 2–3 minutes to combine flavors and release juices.

2. Preheat the barbecue to medium-high (350–400°F), making sure grill is well oiled or sprayed.

3. Add roasted red peppers to the saucepan and continue heating another 2–3 minutes, stirring fruit and peppers together. Remove the pan from the heat, then add tequila and stir. Put the pan back on the burner and, using a long charcoal lighter, light the edge of the dish. While it's still flaming, add the fresh lime juice and then sprinkle on the cilantro. Remove from the burner, cover, and let cool until needed for the marlin.

4. Lightly brush marlin steaks with olive oil and season lightly with salt and pepper. Place the marlin steaks on the hot grill and cook 2–3 minutes per side, until the fish is just lightly browned, the outside flakes easily, and the inside is still opaque.

5. Serve the grilled marlin on a warm plate with a generous 1–2 tablespoons of the mango-pineapple relish on top of each steak.

Smoked Marlin Pie

Marlin is very much like swordfish, but with a slightly tougher texture. The fillets here should be very flavorful while giving a bit of chew.

Serves 4–6

2–2¼ pounds new or red potatoes, peeled and cut into ¼-inch dice

1 carrot, finely minced

2 stalks celery, finely minced

1 cup shredded cheddar or Swiss cheese

Zest of 1 lemon

½ teaspoon red pepper flakes

4 sprigs fresh flat-leaf parsley, minced

1 pound smoked marlin fillets, skin off and boned

1 pound smoked haddock, cod, or trout, skin off and boned

8 ounces large raw shrimp, peeled and roughly chopped

Juice of 1 lemon

2 tablespoons olive oil, divided

2 ripe tomatoes, quartered

2 tablespoons butter, room temperature

3 tablespoons cream or half-and-half

1. Place a stockpot of salted water (2 gallons water with 2 tablespoons salt) on the stove top or barbecue side burner and bring to a boil.

2. Add diced potatoes to the boiling water, cooking until they just begin to soften, about 10–12 minutes.

3. In a sprayed or buttered roasting pan, spread carrots, celery, cheese, lemon zest, red pepper flakes, and parsley and stir to mix.

4. Cut the marlin and haddock into bite-size chunks and add to the pan, along with the shrimp. Squeeze lemon juice over the fish and shrimp, and drizzle with 1 tablespoon olive oil. Add the quartered tomatoes.

5. Drain the cooked potatoes, mash them with the butter and cream, and then spoon into the pan, covering the vegetables, cheese, fish, shrimp, and tomatoes.

6. Drizzle the contents of the pan with the remaining olive oil, then place the pan in the oven or barbecue for 40 minutes; the mashed potatoes on top should be browned and crispy when done.

7. Serve with sautéed squash and onions and fresh cornbread.

Mackinaw Island Fried Perch with Homemade Tartar Sauce

Yellow perch are the primary commercially caught fish in all the Great Lakes as well as many smaller lakes in the United States and Canada. They are fished from Lesser Slave Lake and the Hudson Bay region in Canada, down through the Great Lakes to Kansas, Iowa, Illinois, Indiana, and Pennsylvania, and as far south as South Carolina.

Serves 4

1. Mix all the ingredients for the tartar sauce in a bowl, and store in a covered container in the refrigerator until needed. This recipe makes about 1½ cups of tartar sauce.

2. Remove pin bones from the perch fillets with needle-nose pliers.

3. Dust the fillets on both sides with rice flour, gently pressing the fillets into the flour so both sides have a light coating. Place on a plate, cover, and let sit while you proceed.

4. In an electric frying pan at 365°F or a skillet on a medium-high stove-top burner, heat 1 tablespoon of butter at a time until it melts, and add ½ teaspoon oil (to prevent butter from burning).

5. Fry a few fillets at a time until both sides are browned, about 5–6 minutes. turning once. Remove to a plate covered with two layers of paper towels to drain, keeping the fillets warm. Remove tartar sauce from refrigerator while fish is draining to slightly warm it.

6. Lightly sprinkle the perch fillets with a pinch of salt and a dash of pepper and serve with the tartar sauce.

Tartar Sauce
1 cup mayonnaise
½ cup chopped dill pickles
1 teaspoon capers, chopped
2 teaspoons Dijon mustard
2 teaspoons chopped shallots
2 tablespoons chopped scallions
2 teaspoons lemon juice
6 drops Tabasco sauce, or more to taste
Salt and pepper to taste

2 pounds perch fillets
½ cup rice flour
½ cup butter
2 tablespoons peanut oil
Kosher salt
Freshly ground black pepper

Lake Perch in Lemon-Caper Sauce

Fresh perch never smells fishy, and the flesh will give slightly when you press it with a finger and then spring back into shape. The meat is flaky and very mild flavored.
Serves 4

½ cup flour
1 teaspoon seasoned salt
½ teaspoon freshly ground
    black pepper
Pinch of red pepper flakes
2 pounds lake perch fillets
¼ cup butter
1 tablespoon olive oil
2 cloves garlic, minced
2 tablespoons dry white wine
Juice of 1 lemon
1 cup half-and-half
3–4 tablespoons capers, lightly
    chopped
Zest of 1 lemon
2 tablespoons minced fresh parsley
1 teaspoon savory
1 tablespoon minced fresh
    tarragon
Kosher salt
Freshly ground black pepper
1 lemon, thinly sliced, for garnish
1 lime, thinly sliced, for garnish

1. Mix flour, salt, black pepper, and red pepper flakes in a brown paper bag. Drop perch fillets into the bag one at a time, and shake to lightly flour. Remove the fish, shake off the excess flour, and set aside until all the fillets are floured.

2. Melt butter in large sauté pan, then add the fish several fillets at a time and cook 2–3 minutes per side. Remove the fillets from the pan and keep warm.

3. Add olive oil and garlic to the pan and cook until garlic is tender, about 2 minutes. Add white wine and lemon juice and heat over medium heat to reduce the liquid by one-third. Add half-and-half, capers, and lemon zest and heat until sauce thickens slightly, then stir in parsley, savory, and tarragon and season with salt and pepper.

4. Place the fish fillets on a heated platter, drizzle with some of the sauce, and garnish with lemon and lime slices. Serve remaining sauce at the table.

Dorothy's Cracker Crumby Perch

You can, of course, use any favorite cracker in this recipe, but this is the way my mother taught me to cook fish thirty years ago, and both the crackers and I are still around. In Michigan, where we lived, perch was the fish we caught from our local lakes and ate, hence a lifelong affection for these small, tasty fish.

Serves 4

2 eggs
½ cup half-and-half
2 cups Ritz cracker crumbs
½ teaspoon lemon or citrus salt
¼ teaspoon dried basil
½ teaspoon dried thyme
¼ teaspoon marjoram
¼ teaspoon freshly ground
    black pepper
1 pound lake perch fillets
Olive oil for frying

1. In a flat, wide pan, whisk together eggs and half-and-half.

2. In another flat, wide pan, combine cracker crumbs, lemon salt, basil, thyme, marjoram, and pepper.

3. Dip the perch in the egg mixture, then gently press into the crumbs, making sure both sides are covered with the crumbs.

4. In a large skillet over medium heat, sauté the perch in batches, 2 or 3 fillets at a time in 1 tablespoon olive oil, making sure they are not crowded in the pan. Cook until fillets are browned on both sides, about 3 minutes per side, and flake easily with a fork.

5. Serve with creamed corn and garlic toast.

Pacific Northwest Cedar-Plank Salmon

Untreated cedar wood, when used for cooking, actually becomes a natural flavoring. Native Americans would attach meats directly to a slab of wood and lay it against hot stones or the outside of the fire ring. To cook the large fillet of salmon we use here, you need to use a large cedar plank, or several regular cooking planks placed side by side.
Serves 4–6

1 4–5 pound fresh salmon fillet, boned with skin on
2 tablespoons soy sauce
2 teaspoons balsamic vinegar
2 tablespoons honey
1 teaspoon freshly grated ginger
1 tablespoon freshly minced garlic
2 tablespoons chopped green onions, green part only
4 tablespoons extra-virgin olive oil, divided
1 teaspoon French Fleur de Sel flakes
Freshly ground black pepper

1. Soak cedar plank 2–3 hours in hot water. Drain briefly, pat top of the plank dry, brush it with 1 tablespoon olive oil, and set aside.

2. Place salmon in a shallow baking dish. In a mixing bowl, combine soy sauce, vinegar, honey, ginger, garlic, green onions, and 3 tablespoons olive oil and stir to mix well. Pour half of the mixture over the salmon and let marinate 30 minutes, turning the fish once or twice.

3. Preheat a charcoal grill to 400–450°F, banking the briquettes or coals around the perimeter of the barbecue. In the center, place a large metal pan filled 2 inches high with water. Fill a spray bottle with water and keep handy to douse flare-ups.

4. Remove the salmon from the marinade and drain, discarding the marinade.

5. Place the salmon skin-side down on the plank, season with $1/2$ teaspoon salt flakes and several healthy grinds of pepper. Place the plank in the middle of the grill rack over the water pan.

6. Close the lid and cook 20–25 minutes, basting 2 or 3 times with the remaining marinade, until the fish is cooked: white fat will bubble to the surface, the edges will just start to turn brown, and the center will be medium-rare. Near the end of cooking, the plank may flare up around the edges. This is okay— just spray with water to douse the flames and continue cooking.

7. Remove the plank from the barbecue and place it directly on a serving tray. If you use a metal spatula to cut the salmon in pieces and lift it off the board, the skin from the salmon should remain on the board. Drizzle the remaining marinade over the salmon, sprinkle with $1/2$ teaspoon more of the Fleur de Sel flakes, and serve.

Potato-Salmon Bake

This salmon and potato bake recipe is a great way to use up leftover salmon steaks or fillets, and makes a tasty brunch or dinner. You can use red, baking, or other varieties of potatoes, but the flavorful rich taste of Yukon Gold works perfectly with the subtle salmon flavors.

Serves 6–8

1. Preheat the barbecue or oven to medium-high (350–400°F).

2. In a large bowl, combine salmon, onions, artichoke hearts, eggs, milk, 1/2 teaspoon salt, thyme, dill, and pepper and mix well.

3. Layer half of the potato slices on the bottom of a greased 2 1/2-quart baking dish or casserole. Sprinkle with 1/2 teaspoon salt and drizzle with 1/4 cup melted butter. Spread half of the salmon mixture over the potato layer. Add another layer of potatoes, sprinkle with 1/2 teaspoon salt, drizzle with 2 tablespoons butter, and cover with the remaining salmon mixture. Drizzle the remaining 2 tablespoons butter and the fresh lemon juice.

4. Bake, uncovered, 70–80 minutes or until the potatoes are tender. Remove from the oven and let stand 5 minutes before serving.

3 cups salmon pieces, skin removed
1/2 cup chopped sweet onions
1/2 cup chopped artichoke hearts
4 eggs, beaten
2 cups milk
1 1/2 teaspoons kosher salt, divided
1/4 teaspoon thyme
1/4 teaspoon dried dill
1/8 teaspoon freshly ground
    black pepper
6 cups thinly sliced Yukon Gold
    potatoes, unpeeled
1/2 cup melted butter, divided
2 tablespoons fresh lemon juice

Kate's Four-Fish Chowder

Perhaps the best chowder I've ever eaten, this was cooked for my *Ready, Aim… Grill* TV series during a trip to Alaska, where we used absolutely fresh fish right from the chilly Pacific waters.

Serves 6

3 cups tomato juice
½ cup chopped onion
½ cup thinly sliced celery
1 teaspoon garlic granules
¼ teaspoon dried marjoram
½ teaspoon dried oregano
¼ teaspoon dried savory
¼ cup dry red wine
1 cup sliced mushrooms
½ pound smoked black cod, cut into 1-inch cubes
½ pound ling cod, cut into 1-inch cubes
½ pound boneless halibut, cut into 1-inch cubes
½ pound boneless salmon, cut into 1-inch cubes
2 tablespoons grated Parmesan cheese
Parsley sprigs for garnish
1 lemon, cut into 6 wedges

1. Preheat the barbecue or oven to 375°F.

2. Combine tomato juice, onion, celery, garlic granules, marjoram, oregano, and savory in a large stockpot or dutch oven. Simmer on a barbecue side burner or stove-top burner, covered, for 20 minutes.

3. Stir in wine and mushrooms and simmer 5 minutes or until the mushrooms are soft.

4. Add black cod, ling cod, halibut, and salmon and simmer, covered, 5 minutes or until fish is just cooked.

5. Ladle the chowder into a bowl. If you have a round sourdough loaf handy, cut out the middle and use the bread as a bowl; otherwise, a large chowder bowl will suffice. Sprinkle with Parmesan cheese and parsley, and serve with lemon wedges.

Coho Cakes

You can, of course, use other varieties of salmon in this recipe—it's just that my brother Grant, who lives in British Columbia, introduced me to these delicious cakes in which he used coho salmon.

Serves 4–6

Garlic Mayonnaise

¾ cup mayonnaise

1½ cloves garlic, finely minced

1 tablespoon lemon juice

1 teaspoon freshly grated
    lemon zest

¼ teaspoon paprika

2 large russet potatoes, peeled
    and cut into large chunks

3 tablespoons olive or vegetable
    oil, divided

1 pound coho salmon fillet

½ teaspoon kosher salt

Freshly ground black pepper

4 green onions, green and white
    parts, sliced thinly

1 bunch fresh dill, finely chopped

1 egg, lightly beaten

Panko bread crumbs

1. Combine the garlic mayonnaise ingredients in a food processor and pulse to completely blend. Pour into a covered container and refrigerate.

2. Boil or steam the potatoes until tender when pierced with a fork, about 12–15 minutes. Remove from the pot or steamer, drain, and mash together.

3. In 1½ tablespoons oil, in a large nonstick skillet over medium-high heat, sear the salmon fillet on both sides just so it's cooked through, about 2–3 minutes per side. Remove the fillet to a paper towel to drain off oil.

4. Place the potatoes in a large bowl and add salmon, salt, and pepper; stir well to break up salmon and fully incorporate into the mashed potatoes. Add green onions, dill, and egg, and stir to completely mix.

5. Divide the mixture into 4–6 parts, and with your hands form into 4–6 large thick cakes. Add some panko bread crumbs if the mixture is a little loose and won't hold its shape.

6. In a large skillet, heat the rest of the oil and sauté the salmon cakes until they are golden brown on both sides and completely heated through.

7. Bring the garlic mayonnaise to room temperature and serve with the salmon cakes.

Norwegian Gravlax

Marinated salmon made the Scandinavian way is a wonderful appetizer, or cut it into strips and serve atop a salad.

Serves 4–6

1½ pounds fresh salmon fillet
¼ cup aquavit (or tequila, cognac, or dry sherry)
⅛ cup salt
⅛ cup sugar
1 tablespoon crushed white peppercorns
1 bunch fresh dill, chopped

Mustard Sauce
⅛ cup Dijon mustard
1 teaspoon dry mustard
1 tablespoon white vinegar
⅛ cup vegetable oil
1 tablespoon sugar
⅛ teaspoon salt
1 tablespoon heavy cream
3 tablespoons finely chopped fresh dill

1. Place salmon fillet flesh-side up in a glass baking dish.

2. Combine aquavit, salt, sugar, crushed peppercorns, and dill, and rub this mixture into the salmon flesh.

3. Cover the fillet with foil and place a heavy plate on top of the fish and weigh it down with several cans of soup on top of the plate to compress the fish.

4. Refrigerate 2–3 days, turning the fish over twice a day and basting both sides with the accumulated liquid marinade, while keeping the weight on the fish.

5. When the salmon is cured, remove it from the pan and scrape away the curing mixture; refrigerate covered until ready to serve.

6. Combine the mustard sauce ingredients. Slice the gravlax and serve with toast or crackers with the sauce on the side.

Smoked-Grilled Whole Salmon

I often use soaked wood chips or sawdust to add smoke to fish or meats that I barbecue. Presoak a handful of chips and fold into an aluminum foil envelope (see step 1 below). Place directly on the coals and you've got a good source of smoke for your grilling.

Serves 8–10

½ cup alder wood chips
1 (5–7 pound) whole salmon, head and tail intact, cleaned and scaled
2–3 tablespoons butter, melted
1 teaspoon kosher salt
1 teaspoon freshly ground black pepper
1 teaspoon sage
2 large lemons, thinly sliced
2 limes, thinly sliced
½ medium onion, thinly sliced
¼ cup butter, melted, with 2 tablespoons fresh lemon juice added
Small handful flat-leaf parsley sprigs for garnish

1. Preheat the barbecue to medium high (325–375°F). Presoak the wood chips in cold water, then place on a large (12 x 12-inch) piece of aluminum foil, fold into an envelope, and punch 3–4 holes in the top of the envelope.

2. Cut a piece of heavy-duty foil about 2½ times the length of the salmon. Generously spray grilling or cooking spray down the center of the foil, place the salmon on the foil, and brush 2–3 tablespoons melted butter inside the cavity of the salmon. Sprinkle salt, pepper, and sage inside the cavity, then fill with lemon, lime, and onion slices.

3. Brush lemon butter across the entire surface of the fish, then fold the ends of the foil up over the fish to meet in the center; crimp the foil along the long side edges so it's not too tight against the salmon. On top, where the foil ends meet, fold the ends back to make a small opening the length of the fish, making sure the sides are high enough so juices don't leak out during cooking.

4. Place alder chip–filled aluminum foil package directly on the coals or briquettes and replace the grill. Place the foil-covered salmon in the center of the grill, close the lid, and cook 20–30 minutes or until a thermometer inserted into the thick part of the fish reads 155°F and only a slight hint of translucence remains in the center of the fish.

5. Carefully lift the salmon packet onto a heatproof platter, and fold back the foil so that the cooking liquids are retained. Serve at the table right from the foil package, garnished with parsley sprigs.

Trout in Lemon Cream

The trout should have a clean smell; in fact, newly caught trout should smell vaguely like cucumbers. The skin should still be shining and attractive and the flesh firm to the touch, and the gills should be bright red.

Serves 4

1. Preheat the barbecue or oven to medium-high (350–400°F).

2. Lightly rinse and pat each fish dry with paper towels. Brush the cavities and the outside of the whole fish with lemon juice, sprinkle the cavities with savory, and then sprinkle the fish inside and out with salt and pepper.

3. Place the trout in a lightly buttered or sprayed 13 x 9 x 2-inch baking dish and pour the cream over the fish. Generously sprinkle with lemon zest and seasoned bread crumbs, and bake 5 minutes or until fish flakes easily with a fork.

4. Carefully remove the fish from the baking dish with a spatula, and spoon the sauce over each fillet. Serve with a big scoop of steamed or fried rice, with baked tomatoes on the side.

4 (1½-pound) whole rainbow trout
2 tablespoons lemon juice
1 teaspoon savory
¼ teaspoon kosher salt
¼ teaspoon freshly ground
   black pepper
1 pint whipping cream
2 tablespoons freshly grated
   lemon zest
¼ cup Italian seasoned bread
   crumbs

Mushroom-Garlic Trout

When grilling stuffed trout, a general guideline is to cook for ten minutes per each inch of thickness.

Serves 4

½ cup butter, divided
1 small onion, finely chopped
1 cup finely chopped mushrooms
3 tablespoons freshly squeezed
    lemon juice
3 tablespoons chopped fresh
    parsley
¼ cup panko bread crumbs
1 teaspoon kosher salt
1 teaspoon freshly ground black
    pepper
4 1–1½ pound fresh rainbow trout,
    cleaned

Sauce
½ cup butter
2 cloves garlic, minced
½ cup minced parsley
1 lemon, quartered and seeded

Serving Suggestions
1 lemon quartered or sliced for
    garnish

1. Preheat the barbecue to medium-high (350–400°F).

2. Melt 2 tablespoons butter in a frying pan over medium-high heat and sauté onions until lightly browned, about 4–5 minutes. Stir in mushrooms and lemon juice and cook another 4–5 minutes or until all the liquid has evaporated and the mushrooms are soft and wilted.

3. Remove the pan from the heat and stir in parsley and panko, season with salt and pepper and allow to cool.

4. Spoon the mushroom stuffing into the cavities of the trout; do not overfill. Place each trout on a large sheet of foil, dot with the rest of the butter, and season with salt and pepper. Fold the sheets of foil over the fish and seal all sides with multiple folds. Place the foil packets on the barbecue grill and cook 25–30 minutes.

5. For the sauce, in a small saucepan, heat butter with garlic and parsley, and squeeze in the juice from quartered lemon; stir to mix; set aside but keep warm.

6. Remove the foil packets and open them carefully to check that the fish are properly cooked. If not, leave the packets open and place them back on the grill for a few more minutes.

7. When done, remove the trout from the foil, spoon the butter-garlic sauce over each fish, and serve with additional lemon wedges. Accompany with sautéed potatoes and fresh garden peas.

Shrimp- and Crab-Stuffed Trout

Shirakiku Honey Panko is a wonderful breading for any fish or poultry and is available online at several websites like www.asianfoodgrocer.com, at many Asian grocery stores, and at upscale markets like Whole Foods or the newer Fresh and Easy stores.
Serves 8

Stuffing
½ cup butter
½ cup chopped celery
½ cup chopped yellow onions
½ cup chopped green onions, green and white parts
½ cup cooked crabmeat
½ pound cooked cocktail shrimp, divided
2 cups Shirakiku Honey Panko
¼ pound fresh mushrooms, sliced
½ teaspoon kosher salt
⅛ teaspoon red pepper flakes

16 speckled trout fillets, skin removed
¼ cup white wine
¼ cup melted butter

Serving Suggestion
Butter lettuce or raw spinach leaves

1. Preheat the barbecue or oven to medium-high (350–400°F).

2. In a large skillet over medium-high heat, sauté the onions and celery in butter. Add crabmeat and shrimp and simmer, uncovered, until seafood is warmed through, about 4–5 minutes. Add panko, mushrooms, salt, and red pepper flakes and stir well.

3. Butter two 9 x 13 x 2-inch baking dishes. Place 4 trout fillets in each and top each fillet with 2 tablespoons stuffing. Cover these with a second layer of fillets, pour white wine over the fish, and drizzle with melted butter. Place in the barbecue or oven and bake 30–40 minutes until the fish flakes with a fork and is lightly browned on top.

4. Arrange the trout on a serving platter on top of butter lettuce or raw spinach leaves and spoon the remaining stuffing mixture over the fish.

Trout and Scallop Stew

Another way to serve this is to ladle the stew over buttered noodles or a thick slice of Texas toast that you've buttered and toasted.

Serves 4

1 large onion, thinly sliced
1½ cups tomato juice
2 cloves garlic, crushed
4 small red potatoes, skin on,
    in a small dice
1 green pepper, seeded and diced
1 large tomato, peeled and diced
1 cup diced crimini mushrooms
1 cup corn kernels
¼ cup white wine or water
1 teaspoon kosher salt
4 (½-pound) trout fillets
1 cup small bay scallops
1½ cups fresh green beans

1. Preheat the barbecue or oven to medium-high (350–400°F).

2. Combine onions, tomato juice, garlic, potatoes, green peppers, tomato, mushrooms, corn, wine or water, and salt in a large dutch oven or deep roasting pan. Cover and cook 10–15 minutes or until the potatoes are tender.

3. Add trout fillets, scallops, and green beans to the pan, cover, and cook an additional 10–15 minutes. Let the stew stand for a minute or two before serving.

4. Ladle the stew into deep bowls and serve with thick slices of garlic bread and a green salad.

Mazatlan-Style Walleye Enchiladas

We had these enchiladas in Mexico, except they used dorado instead of the walleye. But since the fish are very similar, we tried some walleye given to us by friends in Minnesota and found this to be one of our favorite fish dishes.
Serves 8–10

1. Preheat the oven to 350°F.

2. Place walleye fillets on a sprayed baking sheet or roasting pan. Sprinkle with salt, pepper, cayenne, and chili powder. Bake, uncovered, 15–20 minutes or until fish flakes easily with a fork. Flake all of the fillets, cover, and set aside.

3. In a large skillet, sauté onions and red peppers in olive oil until tender. Add garlic and cook 1 minute longer.

4. In a large bowl, combine green enchilada sauce, sour cream, mayonnaise, chilies, sautéed onions and peppers, and the flaked fish. Spread 1/2 cup mild enchilada sauce into each of two greased 13 × 9 × 2-inch baking dishes and cover each with 1 cup cheese.

5. Place 1/3 cup of the fish mixture down the center of each tortilla, then roll them up and place seam side down on top of the cheese, filling both pans with enchiladas. Pour the remaining enchilada sauce over the tops of the enchiladas in both pans, and sprinkle with the green onions, chopped tomatoes, and remaining cheese.

6. Cover the pans with aluminum foil and bake 30 minutes. Remove foil and bake 10–15 minutes more or until the cheese has completely melted.

7. Serve with Mexican rice, refried beans, and additional warmed flour tortillas, with bowls of sour cream and guacamole on the side.

3 pounds walleye fillets, boned and skin removed
1/2 teaspoon garlic salt
1/2 teaspoon freshly ground black pepper
1/8 teaspoon cayenne pepper
1 teaspoon adobo chili powder
1 medium onion, finely chopped
1 medium red bell pepper, finely chopped
1 tablespoon olive oil
2 cloves garlic, minced
2 (10-ounce) cans green enchilada sauce
1 1/2 cups sour cream
1/2 cup mayonnaise
2 (4-ounce) cans chopped green chilies
2 (10-ounce) cans mild red enchilada sauce, divided
4 cups shredded Colby–Monterey Jack cheese, divided
24 (6-inch) flour tortillas, warmed
1 bunch green onions, green and white parts, thinly sliced
2 medium tomatoes, seeded and finely chopped

Walleye Jambalaya

If you wish, you can throw some shrimp, crayfish, and/or andouille sausage into the pot to make an even richer, more complex jambalaya.

Serves 6

1½ pounds walleye fillets, skinned
½ cup chopped bacon
1 cup chopped onions
½ cup chopped green or red
    peppers
1 clove garlic, minced
1 cup chicken or vegetable stock
1 (16-ounce) can chopped
    tomatoes
1 (8-ounce) can tomato sauce
1 cup uncooked jasmine rice
¼ cup freshly chopped parsley
1 teaspoon seasoned salt
½ teaspoon thyme
½ teaspoon cayenne pepper
1 tablespoon freshly ground
    black pepper
½ teaspoon filé powder
Dash of ground cloves
Dash of nutmeg

1. Cut walleye fillets into 1-inch pieces and set aside. Preheat the oven to 350°F.

2. In a large stockpot over medium-high heat, cook bacon until crisp. Drain out all but 2 tablespoons of grease, then return the bacon to the pan and add the walleye chunks, onions, peppers, and garlic and cook until tender.

3. Add stock to the pan, then add chopped tomatoes, tomato sauce, rice, parsley, salt, thyme, cayenne, black pepper, filé powder, cloves, and nutmeg and stir well. Pour into a well-greased dutch oven.

4. Cover and bake 50–60 minutes or until the rice is tender and the fish flakes easily when tested with a fork.

5. Serve with thick slices of garlic bread, fried okra, and very cold beer.

Acknowledgments

Heartfelt thanks go out to the following individuals, organizations, and companies without whose help, support, and assistance this book would never have happened.

Adair's Wilderness Lodge, New Brunswick, Larry & Ida Adair

Arndt's Aroostook River Lodge, Maine, Ken & Clare Arndt

Bruce Aidell

Buena Vista by the Sea, Rob & Claire Murphy

Canada Consulate General, Monica Campbell-Hoppe

Canada Rocky Mountain Resorts, Jennifer Gerstenberger

Cape Town Tourism, Nicole Moody

Chef Jordan Asher, The High Lonesome Ranch, Colorado

Chef Walter Staib, City Tavern, Philadelphia

Derek Munn, Outfitter, Doaktown, N. Brunswick

Exotic Meats, USA, Reno, NV

Fish Tales, John & Kam Schroder

Fredericton Tourism, David Seabrook

Gill & Finn, Inc.

High Lonesome Ranch, Texas, Charles & Nancy Hundley

Highliner Lodge, Alaska, Steve & Jill Daniels

Jarden Corporation

Juniper Mountain Ranch, Idaho, Jeff Siddoway

Kruger Optical

L & L Guns, Battle Ground, WA

Lodge Manufacturing

Maine Office of Tourism, Charlene Williams

Mossy Oak

National Wild Turkey Federation

New Brunswick Economic Development & Tourism,

Nicky USA, Portland, OR

Nome Custom Adventures, Richard Bienville

Oregon Spice Company, Patricia Boday

Rafter Six Ranch Resort, Banff, Alberta

Ridgefield National Wildlife Refuge

Rocky Mountain Elk Foundation

Ross Hammock Ranch, Florida, Harold Ross

Saint John Tourism, Sally Cummings

Smoldering Lake Outfitters, Dave Hentosh

State of Alaska Dept. of Commerce & Economic Development, John Beiler

The High Lonesome Ranch, Scott Stewart, Paul & Lisa Vahldiek, Scott Stewart

The Ledges Inn, Doaktown, New Brunswick

The Moose Stops Here, Pat Gillespie

The Radio Kitchen, Mike Reining

Travel Alberta International, Judy Love Rondeau

Trout Unlimited

Wild Game Resources

Nicky USA Inc.

223 Southeast Third Ave.
Portland, OR 97214-1006
(503) 234-4263 or (800) 469-4162
info@nickyusa.com
www.nickyusa.com

From a group of family-owned sustainable farms and ranches across the Northwest comes the finest offering of natural game birds and animals produced anywhere. Since 1990 Nicky Farms has focused on bringing chefs and epicureans authentic American meats like rabbit, quail, fallow venison, Northwest elk, and free-roaming bison (buffalo).

Exotic Meats USA

(Sierra Meat Company)
1330 Capital Blvd.
Reno, NV 89502
(775) 322-4073
Fax: (775) 322-2784
Toll Free (800) 444-5687, ext. 120
sales@exoticmeats.com
www.exoticmeats.com

Since 1992 Exotic Meats USA has been offering the finest game and specialty meats to restaurants, retailers, and consumers. Helpful cooking tips and amazing recipes are only a phone call or mouse click away.

Index

About the Author

Rick Browne is creator, host, and executive producer of the wild game hunting/fishing/cooking show *Ready, Aim... Grill,* which premiered on the Outdoor Channel in 2005 and ran quite successfully for two seasons before Rick took a one-year hiatus to travel around the world for his *Barbecue America 6* series on PBS. A renowned barbecue and grilling expert, he is also the author of *The Best Barbecue on Earth, The Big Book of Barbecue Side Dishes, Grilling America,* and *The Frequent Fryer Cookbook* as well as co-author of *The Barbecue America Cookbook.*

The series will be back on the air on the Sportsman Channel in 2012 as *Grillin' Wild* and will feature Rick cooking up wild game, fowl, and fish on the incredible High Lonesome Ranch in Colorado's Rocky Mountains.

While Rick may be focusing on the world of barbecue these days, his first love was photojournalism. An award-winning member of the Society of American Travel Writers, he has more than twenty-five years of experience to his credit. His writing and photography assignments centering on breaking news, travel, and culinary subjects span the globe and have been published in a wide variety of domestic and foreign magazines, including *Time, Newsweek, People, USA Today, Canadian Living, Islands, Travel Holiday, Reader's Digest, Maclean's, Sunset, Burda, AQUA, Wine Spectator, Geo, Diversion, Saveur, Saturday Night,* and *Travel and Leisure.*

He has appeared on *Fox and Friends, The TODAY Show,* and *Live with Regis and Kelly* and on CNN, and has been featured in *People* magazine and *USA Today.* He has served as a spokesman for Coca-Cola, Bush Baked Beans, Vlassic Pickles, Cattlemen's Barbecue Sauce, Fire Stone grills, PAM Grilling Spray, Bayou Classic, Barbeques Galore, Georgie Boy, Louisiana Hot Sauce, Mexene Chili Powder, Cajun Injector, the National Pork Board, the Propane Education and Research Council, Aidelle's Sausage, and BIC charcoal lighters.

In his frequent role as an editorial food photographer, he has worked with many of the world's greatest chefs, including Julia Child, Jacques Pepin, Martin Yan, Paul Bocuse, Giuliano Bugialli, Marcella Hazan, Jeremiah Tower, Joachim Splichal, Charlie Trotter, Susan Spicer, and Roger Verget. His kitchen/food shots have been published in most of the world's leading food and wine magazines.

Rick is a member of the International Association of Culinary Professionals, the Society of American Travel Writers, the Canadian Barbecue Smokers Association, the National Barbecue Association, the International Bar-B-Que Cookers Association, the Kansas City Barbecue Society, and the World Barbecue Association, and is a founding member of the California Barbecue Association.